CYCLES OF LIFE

✤

MOTHER AND CHILD

✦ SOPHIE BRONCHEAU AND LOUISE, NEZ PERCÉ ✦

◆ KITTY DEERNOSE AND BABIES, CROW ◆

✦ HAVASUPAI WOMAN AND CHILD ✦

◆ ASSINIBOIN WOMAN WITH BABY IN SLING ◆

✦ BLACKFEET WOMEN WITH CHILD ON TRAVOIS ✦

◆ ISLETA PUEBLO WOMAN WITH CHILD ◆

✦ INUIT WOMEN AND CHILDREN, ALASKA ✦

✦ SPOKANE WOMAN AND CHILD ✦

✦ BELLA COOLA WOMAN AND CHILD ✦

◆ WASCO WOMAN AND CHILD ◆

1

THE PROMISE OF YOUTH

Symbolically encompassing the full cycle of human life, a Mimbres ceramic bowl depicting the birth of a child was ritually "killed" by piercing prior to being interred as a burial offering. The 11th-century Indians of New Mexico's Mimbres River valley believed such holes allowed the spirits of the painted figures to accompany the deceased to the afterworld.

As dawn broke over the Sangre de Cristo Mountains in northern New Mexico, the Tewa infant was brought forth to greet the rising sun for the first time. Four days had passed since his birth and it was time for him to be given a name that would incorporate him into the rich and complex world of his people.

During the night, the woman who had delivered the baby—known as the "umbilical cord cutting mother"—had assembled numerous sacred items, including a variety of *xayeh,* manifestations of ancestral souls in the form of seashells, axheads, arrow points, and fragments of white quartz called "lightning stones." She had rubbed the stones together to make sparks in an attempt to bring rain, for rain was a sure sign among the pueblo dwellers that their deities were pleased. Most important of all the items assembled for the occasion were the two perfect ears of corn she carried, one blue and the other white, because they represented Blue Corn Woman Near to Summer and White Corn Maiden Near to Ice, the original mothers of the tribe.

In the beginning when there was no death, the Tewa dwelt beneath a lake "far to the north." One day, the two spirit mothers asked a man to find a way out of their watery home. The man searched the north, west, south, and east, in that order. He found only mist and haze, so the mothers suggested he go above. Predatory animals and carrion-eating birds attacked him, but the hostility of the beasts soon turned to friendship. They painted the man's face black, tied feathers in his hair, cloaked him in deerskin, and gave him a bow and arrows. He returned to the Tewa as Mountain Lion, the Hunt Chief, and he divided the population into Summer People, who would grow crops and gather wild plants, and Winter People, who would kill game. To each group, he gave a chief who would look after the people. The Summer and Winter chiefs then sent six pairs of spirit brothers to explore the earth in all directions, including above and below its surface. The brothers, known as Towa é, discovered mountains to the north, west, south, and east. Atop each peak was an earth navel, or sacred center, to channel blessings to the people. With handfuls of mud, the Towa é built flat-topped hills in front of the mountains.

At length, the mud of the hills hardened, and the people emerged from the lake. With the Towa é watching over them from their mountain aeries, they began the long trek southward. But death and evil existed outside their primordial home, and four times the Tewa returned beneath the waters to create institutions that would bring them into a state of perfect balance and harmony with the rest of creation. These additions included medicine men to guard against witchcraft and to keep the people well, sacred clowns to amuse them, a scalp chief to bring success at war, and a women's society to assist him and care for the scalps.

With the community now complete, the Tewa resumed their migration, following the course of the Rio Grande southward. They stopped and built villages from time to time, but ultimately disease forced them onward. Separating into six groups, they journeyed farther down the Rio Grande until they reached a 20-mile-long stretch of river valley, north of present-day Santa Fe. Here each group halted and built an adobe village. Each of the six villages had its own earth navel and consisted of both Summer People and Winter People, with a Summer chief to guide them during the seven-month-long growing season, and a Winter chief during the five months of hunting. Each community had medicine men and clowns as well as human counterparts of the Towa é to act as mediators between the religious leaders and the ordinary people. It was into this all-encompassing social and moral order made up of human beings and spirits, and into this landscape surrounded by sacred boundaries, that the newborn was about to be initiated.

Bright rays danced on the peaks as the cord cutting mother took the infant in her arms, along with the two ears of sacred corn. With a small broom, an aide made a sweeping motion over the child, gathering in the spirits' blessings. Then the cord cutting mother offered the new life to the six directions. As she turned, she prayed: "Here is a child who has been given to us. You who are dawn youths and dawn maidens. You who are winter spirits. You who are summer spirits. We have brought out a child that you may bring him to manhood and womanhood, that you may give him life and not let him become alienated. Take therefore [the child and the corn]. Give him good fortune we ask of you."

The first gift for a Hopi infant, this "putsqatihu," or flat kachina, is also called a cradle doll. A carved depiction of Hahay'iwuutti, the Mother Kachina, the doll is a protective charm for both sexes. For a little girl, it also represents hope that she will grow up healthy and have strong children of her own.

A Navajo child's first laugh is followed by a ceremonial giveaway of foodstuffs such as coffee, fruit, salt, and assorted canned goods. After the ceremony, children are allowed personal possessions of their own—starting with small items of jewelry.

Her prayer finished, the woman spoke the child's name—words that would never be uttered outside the Tewa community. The ceremony was over. The infant had been brought from a state of darkness, in which he had no identity, to the status of a human being, a child of his people. With this ritual, the baby took his first step along the Tewa path of life. It was the first of many rites of passage he would experience, each providing greater understanding of Tewa tradition until his soul rejoined those of his ancestors—at the stone shrines in the four cardinal directions, on the flat-topped hills made by the Towa é, or on the mountaintops, depending on the status he had attained in life. The Tewa call this path *poeh,* a word that evokes the emergent path their ancestors trod when they came up onto the earth's surface from the dark underworld where they first dwelt.

A stone amulet worn by a little Blackfeet girl was considered to have protective properties and the power to give the young wearer luck for life.

Although different in detail, the traditional life paths of all Native Americans are remarkably similar in essence. All are rooted in wondrous stories of creation that explain not just tribal origins, but the structure and order of reality itself. Consequently, each Indian culture believes that its own particular customs and institutions exist in harmony with the natural processes of the entire universe. And at the core of each set of beliefs lies the heartening notion that the road of human life is endless and everlasting, an eternal way that has been followed, as one Arapaho elder expressed it, "since the beginning of the world."

Although life's roadway contains many twists and turns—the Pima and the Papago (Tohono O'odham) of the southern Arizona desert portray it as a labyrinth—everyone returns in some manner to the point from which he or she set off. All Tewa, for example, begin life on the same poeh at their naming ceremony. A short time later, the poeh splits in two, and an individual travels through puberty, adulthood, and old age as a member of either the Summer People or the Winter People. At death the two paths merge once more, as the soul begins its immortal journey to the Tewa nether world from which it came. For some tribes, however, the souls of the dead return through an earthly reincarnation. The Takulli, or Carrier, Indians of British Columbia believe that the souls of ancestors are reborn into their original families. Although the Carrier do not distinguish every child as a reincarnated ancestor, they accord all newborns the respect of having lived a previous existence.

For the tribes of the Great Plains, life's path has always traced a circle. As a Cheyenne elder expressed the view of his people: "The beginning and end of life come together in the East. In the beginning of life there is the child's cry, announcing the new life. And in the end there is the old man's prayer." For the neighboring Sioux, every facet of being possesses a circular dimension. John Lame Deer, the great-grandson of a Miniconjou Sioux war leader killed by United States troops at the end of the 19th century, calls this concept both symbol and reality, expressing

A Blackfeet baby, such as Little Handsome Woman (below), could expect to have at least two names over a lifetime. A girl's descriptive birth name often was replaced by a warlike name chosen to honor a male relative for his battlefield exploits—such as Attacked toward Camp or Killed at Night.

Maternal grandmother Elizabeth Tootsie stokes a blaze that will burn throughout the night. Baking in a pit beneath the fire is "pikami," a traditional pudding of sweet cornmeal prepared for the celebratory feast that will follow the sunrise naming ceremony.

Wrapped snugly in a woven blanket, 20-day-old Duane Ferren Tootsie, also known as Crow Boy, lies next to his ear of Mother Corn. Hopi legend describes the grain as a gift from the gods; it continues to figure prominently in Hopi daily life and sacred rites.

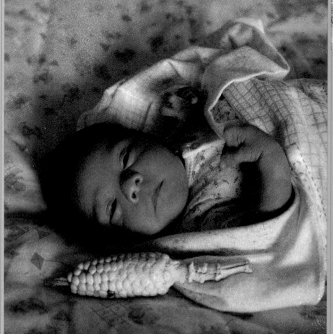

THE POWER OF A NAME

Among the Hopi, bestowing a baby's tribal name is an event of paramount importance conducted by the most experienced and wisest of family members, the elders. Thus did the senior women of the family preside over the naming of Duane Ferren Tootsie, whose ceremony in 1980 is pictured on these pages. For 19 days after his birth, he and his mother remained indoors, shielded from the sun. Traditionally, every fourth day of seclusion, his maternal grandmother washed him with warm water. Finally, on the 20th day, the women of his father's clan honored him with the name Crow Boy.

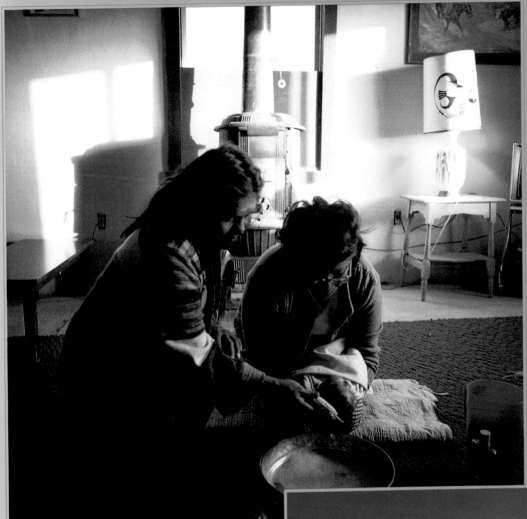

Cradled in the arms of his godmother, Crow Boy sees the dawn for the first time. Beside the pair stands the child's mother, who holds a handful of cornmeal to sprinkle in the breeze as a prayer to the sun.

Paternal grandmother Alice Polacca washes the baby's hair with a carefully selected ear of corn, known as Mother Corn, to ensure long life. Godmother Tonita Hamilton holds the infant. After the grandmother finished washing the baby, each of his paternal aunts repeated the cleansing rite as part of the naming ceremony.

Propped up against the trunk of a tree, a cozily swaddled Apache baby peers out from beneath the shady hood of a cradleboard. Most Indian infants spent a large part of their first year in portable cradles, allowing their mothers to transport them readily and set them down safely in any convenient spot.

After outgrowing the cradleboard, an Apache child graduated to a carrying jacket, a big buckskin pouch with holes for head and arms. Often decorated with the charms that had been attached to the cradle, the jacket could be hooked by the handle to a saddle horn for horseback journeys.

the harmony of life. ''Our circle is timeless, flowing,'' he explains. ''It is new life emerging from death—life winning out over death.'' To these warriors and buffalo hunters, the sky, the earth, and the stars were round. The whirling movement of the wind traced multitudinous circles. Always repeating their endless rhythms, the seasons sketch the same pattern. Herein lay power. ''Everything the power of the world does is done in a circle,'' the famous Oglala Sioux holy man Black Elk once remarked. ''The life of man is a circle from childhood to childhood, and so it is in everything where power moves.''

For Native Americans, power meant the spiritual power of the divinities that dwelt everywhere—in the earth and sky, in rocks and rivers, in great herds of buffalo and green stalks of corn. As Indians journeyed along life's earthly trail, they appealed time and again to the spirits for help and guidance. "To us, the spirit world seemed very near, and we did nothing without taking thought of the gods," said a modern Hidatsa, whose ancestors once lived in earthen lodges along the Missouri River in present-day North Dakota. "If we would begin a journey, form a war party, hunt, trap eagles, or fish, or plant corn, we first prayed to the spirits."

Only by consulting the spirits at each juncture could an individual's safety and happiness be secured. In various tribes, not only was a child's naming consecrated ceremoniously, but a baby's first laugh, first step, or first haircut might also call for sacred rites. About the age of puberty, adolescent boys and girls were initiated into adulthood, often with elaborate ceremony. The middle years brought more rituals, sometimes connected with membership in various secret societies, organized for all sorts of community purposes, including war, healing, recordkeeping, rain bringing, and the dramatization of tribal legends. With death came yet another series of rites, easing the passage of the soul into the spirit world.

The life road of the Indian, however, was more than a series of age-related milestones, one following the other. Rather it was a continuous process of spiritual development, an unending quest for knowledge and wisdom that began in childhood when youths were first introduced to the established ways of the people.

In most tribes, the family was the chief source of education. Within its folds—often stretched wide to embrace a variety of kin, including grandparents, aunts, uncles, cousins, and in some instances entire clans—children learned proper conduct, as well as the myriad tasks and skills they would need to take their place as adults and ensure the continued welfare of the community. "Without the family we are nothing," explained a modern Pomo Indian. "In the old days before the white people came, the family was given the first consideration by anyone who was about to do anything at all. We had no courts, judges, schools. The family was everything, and no man ever forgot that. Each person was nothing, but as a group joined by blood, the individual knew that he would get the support of all his relatives if anything happened."

The older members of the family, particularly grandparents, spoke to youngsters about community traditions and values at an early age. In general, Indian children learned to admire industry and scorn laziness; to emulate the courage of legendary heroes; and to be kind, generous, and respectful of elders. Youngsters were expected to listen vigilantly and to

CHILDREN OF PRIVILEGE

All Native American cultures cherish their children, but certain youngsters have by custom been singled out for lavish attention. Among the Blackfeet of the Northern Plains, such a fortunate youth was known as *minipoka*. "Outstanding children, that's what they are," explained one member of the tribe. "I was my father's favorite, his minipoka," another recorded. Usually the adored child of a wealthy family, the chosen boy or girl was pampered with praise and elaborate gifts from friends and relatives. Such presents have traditionally included miniature tipi covers, toys, fancy clothes, and stand-up bonnets such as that worn by the son of Big Face Chief, seen at left. In return for such favors, a minipoka was expected eventually to assume an important role in the ceremonial life of the tribe. A Sioux baby from a distinguished family received the elaborate pair of fully beaded moccasins, complete with beaded soles, shown below.

hold their tongues, for by remaining silent they opened themselves up to communication with the spirits. "You don't ask questions when you grow up," a Keres Indian of the Southwest once noted. "You watch and listen and wait, and the answer will come to you. It's yours then, not like learning in school." Thousands of miles to the north, a Baffin Bay Inuit gave a similar response when asked how he had gained knowledge. By "being silent in the great lonely stillness of the dark," he replied.

A Hidatsa midwife's medicine bundle includes a rattlesnake bone (bottom) to invoke the snake's power. Midwives carried such talismans along with an array of herbal analgesics. According to one Hidatsa woman, a birthing mother given these drugs "was soon delivered, without a great deal of pain."

Indians traditionally attributed human life to a combination of contributions made by man, woman, and the spirits. A child's father was thought to provide bone and other hard substances, while the mother contributed the flesh and blood. Other elements might come from the tribe's legendary homeland where the souls of ancestors resided. Breath was usually considered to be a gift from the spirit world. Some tribes believed that the body of the child came from a special "baby home." The Mandan of present-day North Dakota adhered to the belief that before birth children resided in certain hills that were also occupied by spirits. Many of the peoples in the Pacific Northwest held a similar view, envisioning the infants as living in a mysterious spiritual realm until they chose their human parents.

Women, by virtue of their capacity to give birth, were universally thought to have special status and potentially dangerous power. The mere presence of a pregnant or menstruating female might harm important male activities, such as hunting and warfare. As a consequence, pregnant females were frequently secluded from the rest of the community. Even among Indians who did not isolate them, pregnant women observed numerous restrictions on their diet and activities because their conduct during the months of gestation was under-

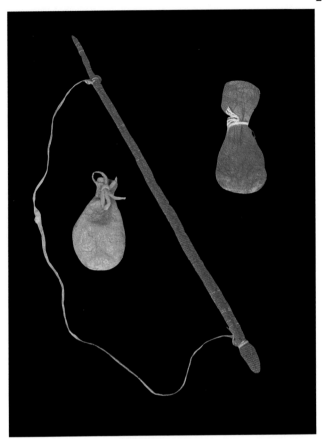

The women of several Plains tribes wore special charms to prevent conception. This Piegan Blackfeet contraceptive amulet consists of a flexible, beaded waistband shaped like a snake and two small hide pouches, one containing yellow paint, the other a small stone shaped like a buffalo, an object that was frequently found in Blackfeet medicine bundles.

stood to affect the ultimate well-being of their children.

While pregnant, women were expected to partake only of those foods with characteristics desirable in a child. Meanwhile, they avoided foods with unwanted traits. Specific taboos varied from tribe to tribe. Among the Cherokee—who originally dwelt in the southeastern part of the country—pregnant women never ate speckled trout; the spotted skin of the fish was thought to create facial blemishes on a newborn. The Apache, on the other hand, believed a pregnant woman should avoid the tongue of any animal, lest it cause her unborn child to be slow in learning to talk. Apache women also eschewed eating eggs, which were thought to make the fetus blind.

Most tribes also recognized various foods thought to hinder—or help—delivery. Abstaining from eating fresh meat was a common custom because it was thought that the blood in the meat might cause miscarriage. For the Cherokee, squirrel was taboo; it might cause the child to retreat into the mother at birth, much as a squirrel scurries up a tree when frightened. Toward the end of her pregnancy, an Apache woman might seek out narrow-leaved plants, such as yucca, to facilitate delivery; eating these plants, however, would mean that her child would always be slender.

In general, not only what a woman ate but also how she behaved and whom she encountered were factors believed to affect the health of her unborn child. A pregnant woman was expected to move briskly when entering or leaving a room; by blocking a doorway, she might slow the birth process. If she stared at a rabbit, she risked giving birth to a child marred by a deformed lip. Should she look upon something ugly, her child might be unattractive. Pregnant women—and often their husbands as well—customarily refrained from tying or fastening cords and ropes, fearing that the motion would constrict the child's umbilical cord. Among the Cheyenne, a woman awaiting the birth of a child refused to string beads or tighten the girth of a saddle on a horse lest her child strangle in the womb. In accordance with Cherokee custom, neither parent was permitted to wear a scarf for the same reason.

The Cherokee also practiced an elaborate ritual meant to safeguard the health of the fetus. At each new moon from the time she felt life stir within her, a Cherokee woman was expected to visit the local river, where particular prayers would be said for her and her child. Before departing from her home, she drank an herbal medicine that was composed of slippery elm bark, pine cones, and various roots and stems. The elm bark, the Cherokee believed, encouraged an easy delivery, while the pine cones, derived from an evergreen, would impart long life to the baby. After imbibing this potion, the expectant mother, accompanied by her husband or mother and a holy man, walked to the riverbank. She brought with her a white cloth, white thread, and two beads, one black and the other either white, symbolizing life, or red, connoting success.

After the party arrived at the riverbank, they spread the cloth on the ground and placed the beads and thread on top of it. Holding a black bead in his left hand and a red or white one in his right, the priest recited an incantation. He extended his arms, and as he spoke, the beads seemed to move of their own accord between his forefingers and thumbs. On the basis of these movements, he offered the family predictions about the pregnancy—the sex of the child, for example, or whether the infant would survive its early childhood. At the close of the ceremony, the woman's husband or mother strung the beads on the thread, wrapped them in the cloth, and handed the bundle to the holy man in exchange for his services. The pregnant woman then vomited up the medicine she had drunk, thereby cleansing herself of any disease that might harm the child in her womb.

In some Indian communities, the prospective father was also subject to taboos. A Delaware man with an expectant wife attached a tiny bow and arrow to his clothing when he went hunting so as to amuse the spirit of his unborn male child and prevent it from frightening the game. If the hunt was unsuccessful, the man assumed that the child his wife was carrying was a girl. The next time he ventured out, he brought along a small mortar and pestle for her spirit to play with. In other tribes, such as the Seminole, hunting by the father-to-be was discouraged altogether, as his presence was thought to bring bad luck to other hunters in the party.

In a number of tribes, women gave birth in isolated lodgings in order to protect the rest of the tribe from the exceptional power of the birth blood as well as

Among Plains peoples, a baby's umbilical cord was put in a beaded pouch and attached to the child's clothing or cradle as a longevity charm. Girls' pouches took the form of turtles; boys' were made in the shape of snakes and lizards. The beading on these Lakota amulets and on the ball (right) reflects the delight relatives took in making small presents for newborns.

to protect themselves and their newborns from harmful spirits and witches that might prey on them. Birth assistants were usually women. Nevertheless, in some tribes, specially trained holy men called upon the expectant mother in her seclusion to perform necessary tasks. A Cherokee medicine man might visit a woman early in her labor, for example, to be sure all the necessities for the event were present. He might also help collect roots and herbs to be used during the delivery. But his main responsibility was to enter each corner of the dwelling and implore the unborn child to "jump down." At the east and west corners, he called for a boy; at the north and south, a girl. Sometimes he circled the room as a precaution against evil spirits who might threaten the helpless infant or the mother, who was weakened from her ordeal.

Among the Navajo, women commonly gave birth at home. When labor began, a midwife, known as "the woman who pulls the baby out," was called to the hogan to prepare the birthing place. Along the west wall of the wood-and-earth hut, she hollowed out a shallow pit, then filled it with warm sand. Over this she placed a clean sheepskin; upon this soft pad the mother gave birth, in a kneeling position. A handwoven sash was hung above the sheepskin for her to grip. Several people assisted the midwife. A sacred singer was often present to offer ceremonial chants to help bring out the child. If labor was prolonged, another religious official, the stargazer, was summoned to determine which spirit had been offended or which taboo broken. Once this was known, yet another singer was summoned to appease the angry spirit.

Although suitable preparations were made whenever possible, women in nomadic or seminomadic tribes often gave birth on the trail. Buffalo Bird Woman, a Hidatsa who shared her knowledge of tribal lore with the anthropologist Gilbert Wilson, recalled the birth of her first baby about 1870. At the time, her band was traveling up the Missouri River to their winter camp. Despite her bulk, Buffalo Bird Woman had walked northward for many days. Finally the band reached its last camping site before fording the river. On a cold and windy day in early November, they pitched their tipis on the hard sand at the water's edge. At midnight, lying on a bed of dry grass and assisted by one of her father's wives, Buffalo Bird Woman gave birth to her son. In the morning, the older woman

bathed the baby with water she had warmed in her
own mouth, then wrapped him in a sack fashioned
from a piece of tent cover. Around his body she
packed soft down plucked from cattails; at his
feet she placed warm sand. Then she bundled
him in a wildcat skin. Later that day, despite
their travail, mother and child crossed the icy
river with the rest of the band.

Native Americans have traditionally attached special power to the placenta, or afterbirth. Great
care was taken with its disposal, lest it fall
into the hands of an evil person who
might use it to practice witchcraft against
the mother or child. The Hopi buried the afterbirths in specially designated *kiwuchochmo,* or "placenta hills," located
close to their villages. Among the Cherokee, the baby's father was expected to carry the afterbirth far from the community, crossing several ridges before burying it deep in the
ground. He then said a prayer asking that his wife bear another child. The
new baby would be born, the Cherokee believed, in the same number of
years as the total number of ridges the father had crossed. The Washo of
the Great Basin region also believed the placenta influenced future child-
bearing. After a Washo woman gave birth, the placenta was bundled together with the severed umbilical cord, wrapped in bark, and buried in
warm ashes. If the mother wanted more children, the package was
placed with the cord on top. If she was satisfied with what she had, the
cord was on the bottom.

The navel cord assumed crucial importance in many tribes. The
Cheyenne believed it represented a child's connection to both family and
tribe; it was placed inside a beaded bag and worn throughout infancy and
childhood, like an amulet. The charm was thought to guide behavior; a
restless child, the Cheyenne often said, was looking for a misplaced navel
bag. The Arapaho also preserved the cord inside a beaded pouch. The
pouch was attached to an infant's cradle; older children and adults carried it on their person. Among the Apache, however, it was the child's
mother who carried the bag with her at all times. Should she mistakenly
discard it, the Apache believed, her child would die.

Multiple births were regarded in a special way, ranging from great joy
to anxiety and fear. Some southern California Indians believed twins had

While many Indians regarded multiple births with fear, Oregon's Cayuse tribe, into which this pair was born, was among those that welcomed twins. The matching pair of umbilical amulets (left) were worn by Lakota twins.

an honored place in the afterworld designated for the most esteemed members of their community. The Iroquois, on the other hand, dreaded twins because it was thought they would grow up to be witches with the mystical ability to see into the future. Other tribes worried that a twin birth upset nature's equilibrium and subsequently starved one baby to death in order to restore proper balance. To the people of Nunivak Island, located in the Bering Sea off the west coast of Alaska, the birth of twins indicated that the mother had had intercourse with two men. Most mothers tried to conceal the multiple birth by killing one of the infants. Among the Twana of the Pacific Northwest, twins were considered to be a disgrace to the entire community. To prevent this calamity, a Twana woman ate no deer meat while pregnant, as deer often gave birth to two young. Women also avoided lying on their backs during pregnancy because this might cause the embryo to split and produce two babies. Twana parents unfortunate enough to have twins often secluded themselves in the woods with their infants for at least a month in shame and humiliation.

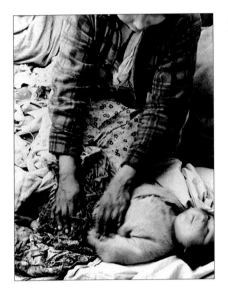

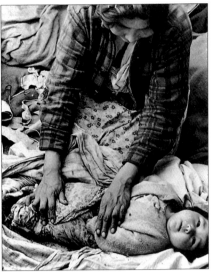

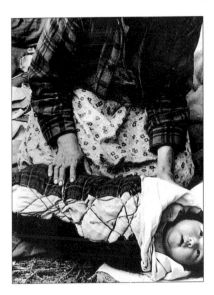

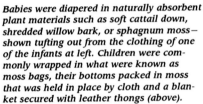

Babies were diapered in naturally absorbent plant materials such as soft cattail down, shredded willow bark, or sphagnum moss— shown tufting out from the clothing of one of the infants at left. Children were commonly wrapped in what were known as moss bags, their bottoms packed in moss that was held in place by cloth and a blanket secured with leather thongs (above).

Even when childbirth was uneventful, Native American mothers and their newborns were often expected to remain in seclusion for a specific period of time. Almost always, they observed some sort of restrictions, both for their own safety and to protect others from the dangerous power that lingered about them after childbirth. Among the Cherokee, for example, a woman who had just given birth was prohibited from cooking. Anyone who partook of a meal she had prepared, it was thought, would become gravely ill. The Hopi followed an even more stringent regimen. For 19 days following the birth of a child, a first-time mother was required to remain indoors until sundown and to abide by severe dietary restrictions. Every four days, she and the baby were ritually washed. Finally, on the 20th day, mother and child were joined by their extended family and bathed once more in the prescribed manner. After this, the infant was presented to the sun and provided with a name. Only then could mother and child take their place in the community.

Ceremonies initiating infants into tribal life ranged from the simple to the elaborate. The Jicarilla Apache ritual for newborns, for example, was particularly intricate. Known as the Long Life Ceremony, the event always took place four days after a child's birth. Before sunrise on the assigned day, a religious elder prepared a bowl of water that had been gathered from four sacred Apache rivers and strewn with pollen and iron ore dust. Then, taking the naked infant in his arms, he prayed for a long life as he sprinkled water over the child's body from head to foot. Next the elder prepared a long strip of deerskin and painted it with red ocher. He held the strip against the baby's body and stretched it out, to symbolize long life. When this part of the ceremony was over, the elder attached a piece of turquoise or abalone shell to the strip, depending on whether the child was a boy or a girl, and set it aside. With the palm of his hand, he proceeded to dust the faces of everyone present with ocher and pollen. When everyone had been painted, the baby was passed first to its father and then to its mother. Finally, the sacred singer wound the piece of deerskin around the infant. Apache children wore the hide until they walked.

An infant's name was always carefully selected, since it would have power over the child's life in the future. Often parents asked a grandparent or a trusted tribal elder to choose the name. Among the Menominee of the Great Lakes region, the naming elder typically spent several months studying the baby's characteristics. His choice was crucial, for the Menominee believed a youngster with an inappropriate name might die. For the Cheyenne, names might be inspired by dreams, unusual animals, or memorable experiences. A Cheyenne who had seen a white turtle while fishing, for instance, might call a baby girl White Turtle Woman.

Names usually revealed the child's gender, either by a suffix attached to the word or phrase or by the subject matter itself. Girls, for example, were frequently named for flowers, boys for predatory animals or birds. Among many tribes, a female child kept her name for life. A boy, however, might acquire a new name during his teenage years, and yet another when he reached manhood, commemorating an important deed or characteristic. One Blackfeet warrior came to be called Behind the Ear because he once shot an enemy in that spot. Another whose horses were all white was called Many White Horses; and yet another who had spoken with the Sun God in a dream was named Brings Down the Sun. As Indians progressed along the path of life, they commonly received new names appropriate to their new status.

Edward Goodbird, the Hidatsa boy born to Buffalo Bird Woman on the Missouri River, once told the story of his own naming ceremony. On the 10th day of his life, Buffalo Bird Woman had called upon her father, Small Ankle, a medicine man, to name her son. "An Indian child was named to bring him good luck," recalled Goodbird. "My grandfather's gods were the birds that send the thunder. He was a kind old man, and took me gently into his arms and said, 'I name my grandson Tsa-ka-ka-sa-ki—Goodbird.' My name thus became a kind of prayer; whenever it was spoken, it reminded the bird spirits that I was named for them and that my grandfather prayed that I might grow up a brave and good man." Goodbird, who lived to be nearly 70, was known throughout his community as a generous man who shared whatever he had, especially with those less fortunate than he.

The health of a child was zealously guarded. Newborn infants were not offered their mother's milk right away, as it was widely believed that the first watery fluid, or colostrum,

As the day-to-day guardians of their children's health, mothers employed a wide array of preventive medicines and charms. This beaded garter was worn by a Mesquakie child of the western Great Lakes region to protect against measles.

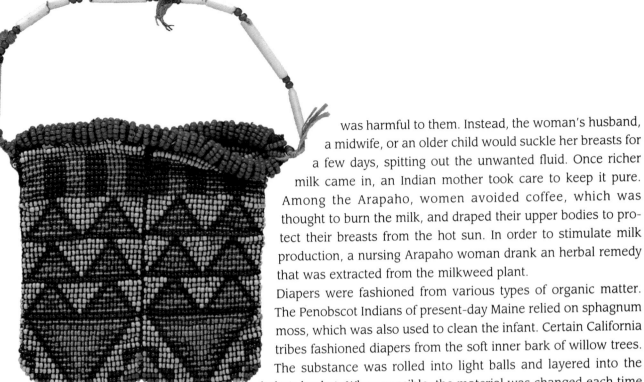

was harmful to them. Instead, the woman's husband, a midwife, or an older child would suckle her breasts for a few days, spitting out the unwanted fluid. Once richer milk came in, an Indian mother took care to keep it pure. Among the Arapaho, women avoided coffee, which was thought to burn the milk, and draped their upper bodies to protect their breasts from the hot sun. In order to stimulate milk production, a nursing Arapaho woman drank an herbal remedy that was extracted from the milkweed plant.

Diapers were fashioned from various types of organic matter. The Penobscot Indians of present-day Maine relied on sphagnum moss, which was also used to clean the infant. Certain California tribes fashioned diapers from the soft inner bark of willow trees. The substance was rolled into light balls and layered into the baby's basket. When possible, the material was changed each time the baby soiled it. Among the Arapaho, babies were covered from the waist down with buffalo manure, well aged and finely ground. The material was held in place by the infant's cradle cover and lacings. Each time the baby was taken out of the cradle, the dried manure was checked—when merely wet, it was aired and dried, then powdered and reused.

The Indians relied on an array of organic salves and medicines to soothe the multitude of ailments from which babies routinely suffer. For one of the most chronic problems, diaper rash, the Arapaho used grease mixed with red clay from a nearby mountain range. Even in recent times, Arap-

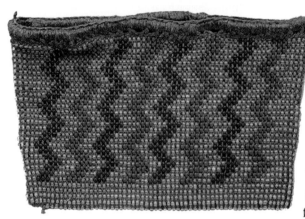

Women of the Mesquakie tribe wore tiny medicine bags such as these under their left arms. If a child was ailing, or going into danger, a mother would take out the medicine object contained in the bag and either fix it under her offspring's arm or wrap it into the youngster's scalp lock. If the woman herself was very sick, the medicine object was rolled into her own scalp lock.

aho women set great store by this ointment. "This red grease is better than the store powder which is used today," a modern Arapaho grandmother once observed. For teething, an Arapaho mother first tried giving the baby a bit of gristle to chew. If that failed, she would catch a mouse, roast it, and rub the meat over her child's throbbing gums.

The Apache developed a wide variety of natural remedies. Facial blemishes were treated either with a mixture of ground moss and mushrooms or with a powder made from the prickly pear cactus. For an earache, Apache mothers rubbed the aural cavity with otter grease. A robin's egg mixed in water was said to help croup; boiled pennyroyal plant was given for fever. A child who exhibited signs of stomach distress might be fed the crop of a wild turkey, ground up and mixed with warm water. The

QUILLED SIOUX CRADLE

Apache considered fearfulness no less an illness than a sore throat. One remedy to cure timidity was to give the child a drink made from herbs and the brain and eye of a woodhouse jay; another was to envelop the shy youth in the smoke of a burning stalk of bear grass.

To stimulate good health and protect against evil spirits—which were thought to prey on the very young—Native Americans turned to the natural resources near their homes. To stimulate talking, for example, Arapaho babies were given eggs and meat from a meadowlark, an especially loquacious bird. Among the Cherokee, a drink brewed from the fibrous roots of the catgut plant was thought to encourage strong muscles. A decoction of wild yellow lily was given to encourage plumpness; a plant known as "eavesdrop" was administered to develop fluent speech. The Apache believed that rubbing a baby's body with the egg and fat of the goldfinch would help it sleep deeply. Illness might be fended off by painting an infant with red ocher and porcupine fat.

Infants raised in temperate climates spent much of their time in cradleboards that were padded with moss or shredded bark. Snug inside this confining device, a baby could be easily hoisted onto its mother's back or, when necessary, set upright under the shade of a tree while she performed her chores. Cradleboards were often objects of beauty, painstakingly crafted from wood, animal skins, and canvas, and elaborately decorated with beadwork or porcupine quills. The Arapaho designed a framework of slender, flexible branches—willow, chokecherry, or sumac—bent into a U shape and held in place with a strip of wood or deerskin. A piece of buckskin or canvas served for the cradle cover. Near the hood that protected the child's head from the elements, the Arapaho sewed a buckskin headband decorated with quillwork—this was said to represent the baby's hair. Pendants, made from bells attached to buckskin strips, were hung on the sides, both for decoration and to amuse the baby. A disk of dyed quills was also stitched onto the cradle cover, near the top; this decoration was said to represent both the sun and the child's head. The colors of the disk were also symbolically chosen—white represented the four corners of the earth; yellow, the light of the sun; red, its heat; and black, the night.

Arapaho cradles were crafted by a small group of women, then presented to the new mother in a ceremony held just after the birth of her child. Before the baby was placed inside, the hood of the cradle was smudged with incense, while the chief cradle maker prayed to the spirits that the child would enjoy a full life. Then the baby was tied into its new

PAWNEE CRADLEBOARD

Although the appearance of infants' cradles varied widely across the continent, most consisted of a soft fabric or skin cover attached to a rigid framework—a basic design dating back at least to the 10th century, when the Anasazi carrier (right) was made. Frames, often highly decorated with sacred or heraldic devices, were made of materials ranging from bark and thin, flat wooden boards to tightly woven fiber basketwork.

bed, where, for the next six or seven months, it accompanied its mother throughout the day. If the mother walked, cradleboard and baby were strapped to her back; if she rode horseback, they hung on the saddle. Once the cradleboard was outgrown by the youngster, it was dismantled during the course of a short ceremony.

As babies reached certain developmental milestones, Native Americans conducted a variety of rituals. Usually joyous events involving much feasting and gift giving, the rituals also played an important role in establishing a child's identity as a member of the tribe. Through these early rites, parents attempted to secure guidance from the spirits. Prayers were offered, entreating the powers to keep the child on the proper path. The rituals were thought to serve a protective function as well, warding off illness, evil spirits, and even death.

The Navajo attached special importance to a baby's first laugh. Four days after the event, the person responsible for eliciting the laughter conducted the Giveaway celebration, consisting of a large meal and gifts for all participants. A Navajo elder remembered with great fondness the story he had been told of his first laugh and the ritual that followed. "I was being held outside in the warm sun," he recounted, "and the sheep were being brought home; I was looking at two little billy goats. They were rearing up with their horns, clashing into each other when, suddenly, I laughed my first laugh. Right away, they said, let's have a little feast for him."

Traditionally, guests were offered the meat left over from the feast. Today, hosts might provide cookies, cakes, and pennies. Each person who attends the Navajo Giveaway is also presented with a nugget of rock salt that has been pressed against the

ANASAZI CRADLEBOARD

HAIDA CRADLEBOARD

CROW CRADLE

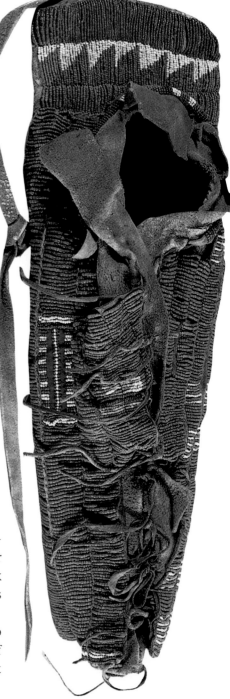

infant's palm. As people accept their keepsakes, they are expected to make statements about the child contrary to what they actually feel. For example, a person might express a wish that the baby grow up to be ugly, so that instead the child becomes handsome. By means of this reverse logic, the Navajo hope to enlist the aid of the sacred clowns, those ritual tricksters who habitually said or did the opposite of what was customary and correct.

The Giveaway ritual was considered an important step in molding a child's character. If it was not held, the Navajo believed, the child would become selfish and unwilling to share. After the event, infants were permitted for the first time to wear adornments, such as bracelets, necklaces, and silver buttons. If the child was a boy, a small piece of turquoise was placed at the head of his cradleboard; for girls, a white shell or bead was used. Amulets made from natural substances were also placed in the cradle with the infant. These charms were designed to encourage desirable qualities. Corn pollen that had been sprinkled on a flying squirrel, for example, was thought to help a child fall down without harming itself. Pollen that had touched a bear would induce strength— although it might also cause the baby to have a bad temper. Another common amulet was a small bug that lives for many months in the bark of the cottonwood tree. Tied to a child's cradleboard, the bug was thought to convey endurance against hunger and cold weather.

The Giveaway ritual established the child as a member of the Navajo tribe. Among other Native Americans, including the Omaha Indians of present-day Nebraska, it was the occasion of the child's first steps that

**CARVED MOHAWK
CRADLEBOARD**

initiated tribal membership. The Omaha ritual, called Turning the Child, was held each spring for all youngsters, girls and boys, who had begun to walk during the previous year. At the designated time, a large tent was erected, with its door flap facing east. On the appointed day, parents and children proceeded to the tent. One by one, holding a new pair of moccasins, each child—barely more than a baby—entered the tent alone.

Inside, a holy man offered a prayer that the child might have a long life. "You shall reach the fourth hill sighing. You shall be bowed over. You shall have wrinkles. Your staff shall bend under your weight," he intoned. Next the holy man turned to a flat stone placed near a fire in the center of the tent and sang an invocation to the winds. Then he placed the youngster on the stone, facing east, and slowly turned it around, to the south, west, north, and east again. Omaha children were cautioned to remain still during the turning; any movement, it was believed, might bring them bad luck. Again the holy man called the wind. At this moment, adults impersonating the four winds stepped forward and whirled the child in every direction. The action, the Omaha believed, inspired strength and self-control. At the close of the ritual, the holy man placed new moccasins on the child's feet and helped the youngster to take four steps, symbolizing entrance into the life of the tribe.

The Tewa mark a child's initiation into one of the two tribal divisions—Summer People or Winter People—with the Water Giving ritual. It is conducted twice a year—once in October by the chief of the Winter People, and once in February or early March by the chief of the Summer People. The day before the ritual, the chief and his assistants prepare a room inside the chief's home. They carefully make a sacred dry painting on the earthen floor by trickling colored grains of sand onto the ground; then they place an altar of fetishes over the painting. On the day of the ritual, mothers and infants gather outside, bearing baskets of flour or bread as gifts. At a given moment, an official utters the cry of a fox, and the Hunt Chief emerges, clad in buckskin and carrying a bow, just as he appears in the Tewa creation story. Pair by pair, the Hunt Chief ushers each mother and child into the sanctuary. There the group chief offers a brief prayer, presses an abalone shell filled with sacred water to each child's lips, and gives him or her a name associated with the group. The infant is now not merely a Tewa, but a Summer or Winter person as well.

Indian children received most of the training they would need as adults during the first decade of their lives. By watching her mother and assist-

ing her around the home, a Native American girl learned what would be expected of her when she became a woman. When she picked her first berries or wild plants, or gathered crops for the first time, she commonly gave them to a female elder who in turn prayed to the spirits that the girl might lead a long life and give birth to many healthy babies. Small boys honed their hunting ability by observing their fathers, uncles, and older brothers, and by tracking small game themselves. They often

The Mesquakie believed that a hawk's feather, such as the one on this scalp-lock ornament, gave a youth courage.

presented their first kills to old men, asking in return for prayers that would make them brave. In their play, children often imitated adult behavior. By telling stories and recounting legends, adults continually reiterated tribal values and instructed the children in appropriate behavior.

While some tribes resorted to physical punishment, most Native Americans exhibited a gentler brand of discipline. In general, a child's spirit was held to be delicate, and Indians took care not to harm it with harsh words or blows. "We like children," an elderly Papago woman once explained. "We talk to them quietly and tell them what to do, but we do not scold. When our children are running about the house, we let them run. If they break something, then that thing is just broken. We do not say anything. We like them to be happy."

The Cheyenne, too, treated their children with tolerance. Young people were held to be close to the spirit world; if they were mistreated, the Cheyenne believed, they might die. Spanking, which was deemed capable of upsetting a child's fragile soul, was avoided. Cheyenne children were given considerable latitude and encouraged to experiment with new activities. Seldom were they punished for mistakes—rather, the Cheyenne excused errors on the grounds that children did not yet know what was expected of them. According to tribal wisdom, the first 12 years of life were critical to a person's development. What a child learned during this period determined whether its life would be easy or difficult.

Some tribes did mete out harsher discipline. The Blackfeet and the

Armed with miniature bows and blunt arrows, two Omaha boys practice their marksmanship by shooting at coins on the ground. Boys were encouraged to play with toys such as slingshots, stilts, darts, and tops in order to develop the quickness and coordination needed for hunting and warfare. Generally they eschewed dolls, although the full warrior regalia on the Kiowa doll (above) mark it as suitable for a little boy.

Toys such as the exquisite ceramic doll securely swaddled on its cradleboard (right), made by the Indians of the southern Colorado River region, and the play tipi of the Blackfeet girl at left were designed to introduce girls to the role of women. From birth, females were directed toward motherhood and domestic duties.

Crow used water to correct misbehavior. "If a child cries too long, they put it on its back and pour water down its nose," a Crow elder explained. "Before long the words 'bring the water' quiet it." Older children who transgressed were punished by having water thrown directly into their faces. Especially for boys, this punishment was thought to be a necessary beginning in a toughening process that would prepare them to be warriors.

The Apache also relied on strong corrective measures, perhaps because they, like the Crow and the Blackfeet, placed an extraordinary value on courage and strength. A small boy who misbehaved, for example, might be punished by having a hole punched in his earlobe with a needle-pointed awl. Whipping was also used to keep children in line. Apache grandparents assumed a large share of the responsibility for shaping a youngster's values and behavior. It was they, not the parents, who administered physical punishment, and Apache children often feared their grandparents. The relationship, however, had other dimensions. Apache children also teased their grandparents, scoffing at their forgetfulness, for example. And they set great store by the traditional tales these older relatives related. So important were a grandparent's stories to an Apache's upbringing that a child might be excused for misbehavior on the grounds that "he had no grandparent to give him the stories."

Traditionally, storytelling was one of the most cherished means of instruction for Native Americans throughout the continent, and all Indian children were continually exhorted to listen to their elders. "One of my favorite memories is sitting down by my grandmothers and hearing them tell us kids the many different myths and legends that have been handed down from my ancestors," a Blackfeet woman remembered. "Just like the fairy tales of other peoples, our legends let childhood imaginations do the impossible."

Early in life, Cheyenne children had both earlobes pierced, a rite symbolizing the child's capacity to listen. The Menominee instructed their children to "sit quiet like a stone, and let thoughts come to you." From toddlerhood onward, Menominee children were exposed to the lore of their people through an endless cycle of stories. On certain prearranged evenings throughout the year, the elders held court around the campfire. The stories they told ranged from uncomplicated tales of everyday life to elaborate creation legends and the exploits of ancestral heroes. Small children might be told a fable about how the skunk came to have its stripe; older ones learned about the origin of their people and the nature of the world. Concealed in most tales was information about the kind of conduct that was expected of young people. During these long evenings around the campfire, the children learned to value bravery, to respect the rights of others, and to cultivate positive relations with the spirits.

The Menominee also lectured directly to their youngsters, beginning at about the age of eight. These instructions covered topics such as marriage, appropriate sexual behavior, and respect for the elders of the community. Children learned about the various natural medicines that were used to cure disease and encourage good health. Because these lessons took the form of gentle, well-meant advice, Menominee children normally accepted the traditions of their tribe and offered little in the way of youthful rebellion.

From an early age, Native American children acquired skills specific to their sex. Boys quite naturally followed in the footsteps of their fathers, uncles, and older brothers. Among the 18th-century Cherokee, for example, two walks of life in particular required many years of specialized training—the priesthood and the ceremonial hunters. Although boys designated to become spiritual leaders of the community generally inherited their right to be candidates, they still had to pass an extensive screening process that weeded out the unfit and matched the chosen with an appropriate sacred calling. Before the training began, parents fasted and ate a special root in the hope of giving their child the spiritual power to excel. The boys themselves also were required to follow dietary restrictions and were forbidden to wander about freely like the other boys of the village. At about the age of nine, the youngsters were assigned to a priest who would reveal to them his knowledge of sacred lore

Naughty Hopi children are disciplined with threats that ogre kachinas, such as the one represented by this doll, might devour them. In some villages, adults dressed in ogre-kachina masks still visit and make playful attempts to kidnap the youngsters.

and subject them to certain physical tests. The child intended to become spokesman for the war chief, for example, could not eat breast meat or the tongue of any animal and was obliged to climb a mountaintop and watch the course of the sun as it passed across the sky, from sunrise to sunset. A single priest might train as many as seven boys at a time. At the end of the course, he foretold each boy's worthiness for certain holy callings by examining a piece of sacred quartz crystal. The priest placed the stone in the sun; if the image of an old man appeared on it, the future success of his protégé was ensured.

The Cherokee were cunning hunters who killed a variety of game. They went after deer, their principal large meat animal, by dressing up in complete deerskins, antlers and all, and luring the creatures to them by making deer noises. In addition to learning to shoot a bow and arrow for deer, bear, and other big game—as well as a hollow cane blowgun for small animals—boys destined to become ceremonial hunters were required to spend as many as four years mastering the sacred observances that opened and closed each hunting season.

Native American boys typically had tremendous freedom. A Sioux father, for example, crafted miniature bows, arrows, and quivers for his son, and instructed the boy in their use. Sioux boys played games emphasizing endurance, strength, and the ability to withstand pain. They also hunted together, tracking and shooting rabbits, birds, and other small game. As soon as a boy could straddle a small horse's back, he was given a pony or colt of his own to ride and look after.

A Sioux girl assisted her mother with household chores, helping to wash dishes, gather wood, and pick berries. By the time she was 10 years old, these tasks were hers alone. She also learned to care for younger children. Even at age six, a Sioux girl might have responsibility for feeding, changing, and amusing a younger sibling. During these years, she also acquired a range of other skills that she would need as an adult. Instructed by her mother, aunts, and any older sisters, she learned to cook, to tan hides, to quill, and to bead. Girls in many other tribes had similar responsibilities at a very young age.

The Yakima Indians of present-day Washington State assigned expert tutors to teach their children. These tutors, who were customarily older relatives, provided the young people instruction not only in practical living skills but also in important spiritual matters. Alex Saluskin, a Yakima born in the early 20th century, has written about his first hunting and fishing trip with his uncle. The older man showed the boy how to kill and

butcher deer and mountain sheep, catch and dry salmon, and gather edible plants. Each day, the young Saluskin purified his body and his soul by taking an early morning sweat bath in a lodge fashioned from fir boughs and reeds, followed by a swim in an icy mountain stream. "At the end of my trip," Saluskin remembers, "I was wiry; probably I could walk for days and weeks if I had to. I had gone through my course of training for survival. I had learned every herb, root, berry, and how to take care of them."

Early morning swims in frigid waters constituted a common toughening stratagem employed by many tribes. In the coldest part of the winter, Apache boys were ordered to jump into the river and then told to warm themselves by shouting. Another procedure used by the Apache was to throw a boy naked into the snow and make him run. Once the boy's circulation was up, he was asked to hold chunks of snow in his hands until they melted. "If you do all the hard tasks," an old warrior once advised his charge, "someday when the enemy shoots you and you fall, though blood comes from your mouth, you will recover."

During the performance of a hunting dance at New Mexico's San Ildefonso Pueblo, a little boy listens intently to instructions being given by an experienced older man whose role is to watch the dancers and come to the aid of those who are in need of help.

Despite the hard work, childhood was a pleasant time for most Native Americans. Maria Chona, a Papago woman born about 1840, recalled her childhood in southwestern Arizona, near the Mexican border. She and her family lived in a shelter made of grass, high up among the hills where the prickly pear cactus grew thick. Every morning the family woke in darkness, for her people considered it felicitous to rise early. "Open your ears, for I am telling you a good thing," Chona's father would say each

Deep inside a subterranean ceremonial chamber, known as a kiva, a Hopi boy is painted as a boldly striped Koshare clown, one of a group of kachinas that burlesques unacceptable behavior as a means of instructing against it. Hopi boys are traditionally initiated into kachina societies between the ages of seven and 10, each youngster sponsored by a respected male who has been selected by his parents.

morning. "Wake up and listen." Each day he urged his sons to go out and run, so they would be swift in times of war. The daughters were told to practice running as well, and to grind corn to feed their men after battle. Bringing water

In the early 1900s, an elderly Seneca woman clutches a young girl with one hand while holding in the other a big double-headed pestle for grinding corn. It was common practice in many Indian nations for the much-respected oldest generation to teach children tribal tradition and lore, as well as techniques for domestic chores, while the youngsters' parents were busy hunting, tending fields, or working at crafts.

was one of their most important responsibilities. The older girls would leave the hut, gather up their water jars, and place them inside fine net bags, which they tied to their backs. Then they would run up into the hills to a water hole red with mud. When they returned, each girl had two jars of water to last her family for the day.

When Chona was small, she stayed at home to help her mother grind seeds and prepare food. During the day, she played with her cousins of the same age. Often they imitated their parents' housekeeping, child rearing, and hunting. Their dolls were made of mesquite leaves, and they pretended to grind corn with a small stone and some sand. The boys would pretend they were hunters, like their fathers and older brothers. The children also ran races on a stretch of desert the men of the village kept clear of cactus thorns. Each winter, Chona and her family migrated south, into Mexico, where her father and brothers hunted deer, while she, her sisters, and her mother gathered the great century plant. When the cholla cactus grew green, the family walked deep into the hills to gather the tender shoots. After the giant saguaro cactus had ripened, they camped in the groves and gathered the red fruit that would be brewed into a sacred liquor to be used in various ceremonies. Chona lived into her nineties. As an old woman, she recalled her early days with pride. Her childhood had bred in her respect for hard work and a reverence for the land.

Childhood for Native Americans typically ended soon after youngsters reached 10 years of age. With puberty would come another round of ceremony and increased responsibility. Few tribes celebrated the end of this happy time. The Tewa, however, stage an important ceremony—the Water Pouring rite—sometime between a child's sixth and 10th birthdays.

Preparations for the ceremony begin 12 days prior to the event. First the kiva—a symbolic representation of the Tewa's ancestral home beneath the lake—is cleaned, and specific adults are selected to impersonate the Tewa deities. Then, during each of the four days before the ritual, the young participants bring gifts to the homes of the adults who will serve as their sponsors. Boys chop and carry firewood; girls grind corn and load it into baskets. In exchange, the sponsors instruct the youngsters in Tewa lore. Finally, on the fourth night, masked adults, impersonating the spirits, visit the kiva. For the first time in their lives, the children are permitted to gaze upon them. Afterward, they receive a ritual bath. With the completion of this ceremony, the carefree, innocent days of early childhood come to an end, and Tewa youths enter into a new phase of responsibility as they pass through the portal to adolescence.

Jagged rocks such as these in the Okanagan Valley of British Columbia have sheltered Interior Salish vision seekers for centuries. Most of the questers sought out commanding landmarks that were thought to be favored by the spirits.

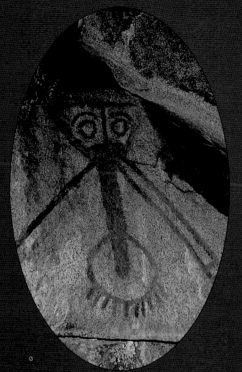

A petroglyph painted below the Okanagan Valley overhang (left) verifies an Interior Salish Indian's vision quest. The drawing probably represents the guardian spirit of the quester.

THE DREAM SEEKERS

Native Americans have traditionally viewed success in life as a gift from the gods. Seeking this gift, countless Indians have undertaken solitary journeys to remote locations in the mountains or forests, where they would fast and pray in the hope of receiving spiritual guidance in a powerful dream. Among several tribes, these vision quests marked the passage into adulthood for adolescent boys. In some communities, the practice endures today.

Although details of the ordeal varied from tribe to tribe, most vision quests lasted between four and six days. After a ritual purification, some Sioux questers spent the entire period in an earthen pit, naked except for a buffalo robe. Crow youths often slept inside a symbolic fasting bed, a stone enclosure facing east so that "the blessings of the morning sun may enter directly" upon them. The most determined seekers resorted to an act of self-mutilation, chopping off a finger joint, for example, or gouging out tiny bits of flesh from their arms and legs as a means of inducing the spirits to take pity on them. Offerings of tobacco and other sacred items were also commonly made. Among the Indians of the Pacific Northwest, repeated bathing in frigid pools was the route to spiritual revelation. The Luiseno of southern California used the hallucinogenic jimson weed to induce a vision.

When a vision did come—usually in the form of an animal, an insect, a natural phenomenon, or some legendary creature—it revealed the dreamer's guardian for life. Seeing an eagle, a bear, a thunderbird, or a bolt of lightning, for example, might imbue a man with particular power. He might be instructed to paint the image of that power on his shield or carry a token of it in his medicine bundle. Henceforth, he was required to observe the obligations and taboos traditionally associated with his guardian spirit.

Many tribes have encouraged their adult members to continue seeking visions as a form of spiritual renewal. As one experienced dreamer once explained, it was only during a dream that "you see something with your inner eyes, with all your soul and spirit."

Accounts of the experiences of individual questers from several tribes, along with photographs of various quest locations, appear on the following pages.

Alpine forget-me-nots and other wild-flowers carpet a ridge along the Wallowa Mountains in northeastern Oregon. When the Nez Percé Indians occupied this region, the range was one of their most popular vision quest sites.

"After going so many suns without food, I was sleeping. It was just like dreaming, what I saw. A form stood in the air fronting me. It was the spirit of a wolf that appeared to me. Yellowlike in color, it sort of floated in the air. Like a human being it talked to me, and gave me its power."

YELLOW WOLF - *Nez Percé*

A swan's-head medicine object honors a Nez Percé guardian spirit. After a creature appeared to an Indian in a vision, he would commonly kill one of its species and keep part of the dead animal as a charm.

The design for this 1930s deer-hide tunic first appeared to Big Plume, a 19th-century Blackfeet warrior, in an adolescent vision quest. The rights to the design were passed down through ensuing generations.

"When my eldest son died, I felt his loss so deeply that I climbed to the mountain's summit and lay there fasting for 10 days and 10 nights. During that time, the spirit of the mountain appeared and gave me a medicine robe. He instructed me how to make the robe and said that if I used it in doctoring I would be endowed with wisdom and power."

BRINGS DOWN THE SUN - *Blackfeet*

Generations of Blackfeet youth have fasted and sought visions in the Rocky Mountains of northwestern Montana. This stand of aspens is in an area called Badger Two Medicine.

On the north shore of Lake Superior, waves pound the base of the Agawa Rocks, a granite cliff that has been an Ojibwa vision quest site for centuries. Accessible only by a narrow ledge, the cliff provides the solitude necessary for communing with the spirit world. The cliff wall is covered with pictographs drawn by young men who wished to record their visions.

"The loon flew out into the lake and brought me a fish to eat and told me that I would have good luck in hunting and fishing; that I would live to a good old age; and that I would never be wounded by a shotgun or rifle. This bird who had blessed me was the kind that one rarely has a chance of shooting. From that time on the loon was my guardian spirit."

—Anonymous Ojibwa from Sarnia, Ontario

Before embarking on a vision quest, an Ojibwa commonly filled a pouch like the one below with an offering of tobacco. Although such bags were usually decorated with the image of their most powerful sky deity, Thunderbird, the quillwork design on this one probably depicts a horse.

Crow warriors often recorded their visions on shield covers like the one below. Since the Crow believe that revealing a dream robs it of its potency, the meaning of this design is unknown. The weasel pelt underneath is a medicine bundle imbued with exceptional power; its owner created it after a weasel appeared to him in a vision.

A rainbow stretches across the sky above the Pryor Mountains in Montana. The range's dense forests and remote outcroppings have been sanctuaries for generations of Crow vision seekers.

"A bear lifted me up so that I could see all the earth. He made me touch his teeth; he had none at all. 'You may jump among high cliffs or do what you please,' said he. 'You cannot die. When you have no more teeth and all your hair is white, you shall fall asleep without awaking.'"

FULL MOUTH BUFFALO, CROW

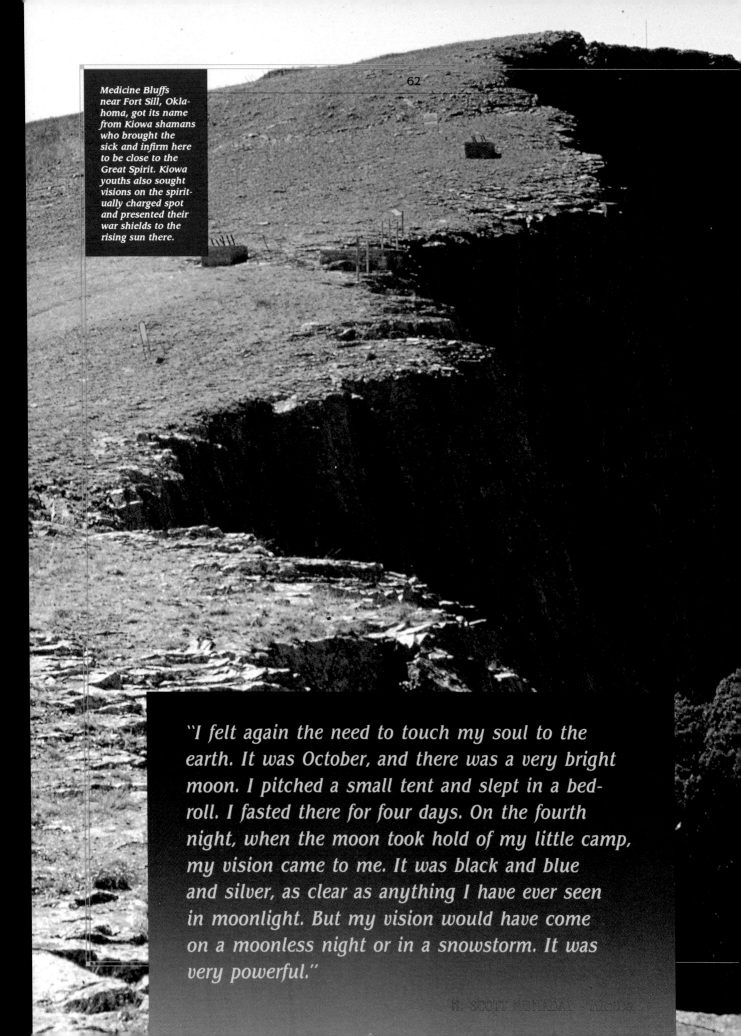

Medicine Bluffs near Fort Sill, Oklahoma, got its name from Kiowa shamans who brought the sick and infirm here to be close to the Great Spirit. Kiowa youths also sought visions on the spiritually charged spot and presented their war shields to the rising sun there.

"I felt again the need to touch my soul to the earth. It was October, and there was a very bright moon. I pitched a small tent and slept in a bedroll. I fasted there for four days. On the fourth night, when the moon took hold of my little camp, my vision came to me. It was black and blue and silver, as clear as anything I have ever seen in moonlight. But my vision would have come on a moonless night or in a snowstorm. It was very powerful."

The design for this tipi cover was conceived by a 19th-century Kiowa warrior who saw the leader of the porcupines in a dream. As depicted on the tipi cover, the nimble beast appeared to the warrior while catching an arrow between its paws to prevent it from piercing its heart.

This Menominee medicine bag was fashioned from beaver skin and embroidered with porcupine quills. Inside were a variety of sacred objects related to the owner's vision and used by him to seek protection and help from his guardian spirit.

Among the Menominee of the western Great Lakes region, boys blackened their faces with charcoal and pushed deep into woods like those shown here to seek a vision. Although the vision quest was optional among some tribes, for the Menominee, it was a crucial part of a boy's journey toward manhood.

"After I had fasted eight days, a tall man with a big red mouth appeared from the east. The solid earth bent under his steps as though it was a marsh. He said, 'I have pity on you. You shall live to see your own gray hairs and those of your children. You shall never be in danger if you make yourself a war club such as I have and always carry it with you wherever you go.'"

—Menominee elder

2

RITES OF PASSAGE

At a ceremony in 1990, an Alutiiq dancer from Kodiak Island, Alaska, whistles a love song on the ivory mouthpiece of a brightly colored courting mask. Traditional Alutiiqs whistle only when they wish to summon the help of benevolent spirits.

Working meticulously in the gray predawn chill of a July morning, a group of young Mescalero Apache men begin erecting a sacred tipi, the *isaanebikugha,* or ''old age home,'' on the tribal ceremonial grounds in south-central New Mexico. The young men lay out the tipi's frame—12 evergreen poles, representing the 12 moons of the year—on the ground like spokes in a wheel. The main structural poles, known as the Grandfathers, receive special dustings of cattail pollen, whose yellow color represents fertility. The young men first lift the primary poles into position, pausing to acknowledge the four cardinal directions. The first Grandfather, on the east, symbolizes the moon and the stars. The second Grandfather, to the south, represents the mountains as well as the sky elements of wind, rain, clouds, thunder, and lightning. The third Grandfather, on the west, stands for the animals. Finally, to the north, the young men lift up the fourth Grandfather. Symbolizing humankind, he is always the last to go up because, as the Mescalero say, ''man is a frail being,'' and the other three Grandfathers are needed to support him.

As the work proceeds, a group of *gutaat,* or ''holy men,'' offer prayers to the Grandfathers. The gutaat have memorized the tribe's entire repertoire of sacred chants and song-stories in an archaic dialect unintelligible to ordinary Mescaleros. After the old age home has been erected, the chief gutaat faces the east and raises his left hand. On his palm he has painted an abstract rendering of the sun. He begins to sing, timing his song so that the last note ends just as the first rays of light shine across East Mountain and strike his palm. This is the signal for several adolescent girls to step forward. Each girl is led to her place in front of the sacred tipi by a *naaikish,* or ''godmother,'' versed in ceremonial knowledge. Dressed in traditional clothing—a fringed buckskin skirt, an elaborately beaded buckskin overblouse, and a large shoulder scarf—the girls kneel on buckskin mats, facing the dawn. Their birth mothers stand behind them, holding burden baskets brimming with food, while their fathers and mothers' brothers take their appointed positions nearby. The singers bless the girls with pollen to ensure that they will one day bring forth strong sons and daughters so that the Mescalero might continue to thrive.

The godmothers bless the girls and the spectators, and are blessed by them in return. Then each girl lies flat on her stomach, facing the east, and her godmother massages her shoulders, back, hips, thighs, calves, and feet, ritually molding her into a strong and healthy woman. A basket, representing the heart of the Mescalero people and filled with sacred grass, pollen, eagle feathers, and tobacco, is brought out from its place of honor inside the old age home. While the singers chant and the godmothers ululate, the girls make four runs around the basket, each circuit bringing them closer and closer to the lodge. The runs represent the four stages of life—infancy, childhood, adulthood, and old age—and reenact the journey of White Painted Woman, the mother of the Mescalero. In the days following creation, she appeared in the east as a beautiful young woman and traveled to the west as an old woman where she disappeared, only to appear again in the east, young and beautiful as before.

A Mesquakie girl who dreamed of a particular animal during her puberty initiation—perhaps a rabbit or squirrel—caught one and then used its pelt as the protective charm above. Women kept fetishes such as these for their entire lives as a means of warding off sickness and sorrow.

Thus begins the most sacred activity on the Mescalero religious calendar—the girls' puberty ceremony. More than a rite of passage, the carefully orchestrated, eight-day-long event is a reenactment of ancient Mescalero history. But it is also a social occasion, and participants and spectators come from near and far to enjoy the four-day public portion of the ceremony that, in addition to its sacred aspects, includes free meals, gift giving, various games, dance contests, and an all-Indian rodeo. During the final four days, the girls go into seclusion with their godmothers and female relatives to receive private instruction about the duties and responsibilities of marriage and womanhood.

The survival of the puberty ceremony is a testament to Mescalero tenacity. The tribe barely endured the travails of the 19th century. Hunted down and incarcerated by United States troops, the Mescalero had dwindled to fewer than 500 persons by 1873, the year President Ulysses S. Grant, by executive order, established a reservation for them in south-central New Mexico. Still fearful of the Apache, the government prohibited the Indians from congregating in groups of more than six—far too small a number to hold a major ceremony. In 1911 the federal government loosened the restriction and decreed that the Apache could gather in large numbers on the Fourth of July. Two years later, instead of celebrating Independence Day as government officials expected, the Mes-

Dancers representing powerful, benevolent beings known as "gaans" perform at the puberty ceremony of a White River Apache girl. As key participants in such rites, these masked dancers drive away evil spirits and sing special chants for the girl in order to prepare her for womanhood.

Wrapped in a robe and crowned with fir branches to ensure good health, an Interior Salish girl is properly attired for her first menstrual period. A girl's spiritual powers were believed to be so potent during her first menses that it was feared she might harm herself if she touched her own skin.

calero took advantage of their new right of assembly to hold the first public puberty ceremony in some 40 years. After the resurrection of their ancient ritual, the Mescalero community began to grow, their population quadrupling over the next six decades to more than 2,000. Many Mescaleros credit the girls' puberty ceremony—which they call "our feast"—with the revitalization of their tribe.

Although few tribes celebrated the advent of menstruation as elaborately as the Mescalero Apache, historically all Native Americans have observed some sort of formalized ritual to publicly acknowledge their daughters' passage into womanhood. Many Indian communities continue these practices today. The transformation of sons into men was also recognized, but not because of any physical changes in the boys. Rather, about the time of puberty, but often several years earlier, male offspring were commonly expected to undergo various kinds of ordeals. The particulars varied from tribe to tribe. Periods of isolation and fasting in the woods and mountains, sweat baths and cold-water swims, the consumption of intoxicating substances, and the rubbing of the body with fish spines and herbs were among the most notable practices. In some tribes, pubescent boys became eligible to join secret male societies and be introduced into the mysteries of the tribe.

The coming-of-age practices were designed to help youngsters attain spiritual power. In some cultures, certain spirits were associated with certain families and could be sought out in particular locations, such as on mountaintops or buttes, or in caves, pools, or waterfalls. The fasts and puberty ceremonies provided the opportunity to make a connection with these spirits. What the young people experienced during

A Nootka girl of Vancouver Island experiencing her first menses announces she is marriageable by wearing a woman's hair style, elaborately decorated braids gathered into two bundles and secured by wool bands. She uses the comb that is pinned to her cloak to scratch her head without touching herself—in accordance with menstrual taboos.

Believing that menstruating women possessed potentially dangerous powers, the Interior Salish of British Columbia confined them to remote branch-and-bark huts such as the one at left. At the time of a girl's first confinement, she ventured outside only at night or in the early morning.

these rites had a deep and lasting influence on their future lives, for in order to begin a productive adult career, every Indian boy or girl needed to establish a positive affiliation with an immortal guardian.

In the lore of the Omaha Indians, the mind of a youth on the threshold of adulthood is said to be "white," a metaphor for the darkness of night passing into the light of day. Having emerged from the incomprehension of infancy and passed through the dim gropings of early childhood, the mind of the Indian adolescent, like the new dawn, is about to enter the bright consciousness of adulthood.

Almost all Native Americans believed that at the onset of her first menses, a girl possessed exceptional power over the persons and things that came near her. Although some cultures ascribed special curing power to the menstrual flow, most Indians considered it a contaminant that endangered weapons, hunting and fishing gear, game animals, cooking utensils, and even certain spirits. As a result, many tribes secluded the girls in a special menstrual hut, usually for four days, but sometimes for several weeks. A few families among the tribes of the Pacific Northwest sent their daughters off for as long as a year or more. During their isolation, girls ate sparingly, took little water, and learned about marriage and the prescribed rules of female behavior—usually from a grandmother or another female relative. Particular emphasis was given to teaching the girls the long series of taboos they would be obliged to observe during every subsequent menstruation. Navajo girls, for example, learned that during their menstrual periods, they could not carry water, go into the fields where crops were grown, or have any contact with children or livestock. Otherwise, they were warned, they could bring harm to themselves, their families, and their communities. The Sioux called this time in a woman's life *isnati,* or "dwelling alone."

Other cultures were equally restrictive. The Winnebago, a Siouan-speaking people from the western Great Lakes region near present-day Green Bay, required their menstruating women to live in lodges scarcely larger than their bodies for the duration of each menstrual period. They were obliged to remain in a sitting position and not look outside the lodge during the hours of daylight. At night, their limited meals were cooked over special fireplaces and served with specific utensils. If they had an itch, they scratched themselves with a special stick for fear that if they touched their bodies directly with their hands they would bring on an illness. The women had to be particularly careful to avoid contact with any sacred objects, such as a family member's medicine bundle, lest the menstrual blood rob the objects of their power.

The only respite from this harsh regimen came after sundown when male suitors were allowed to visit the young unmarried girls. Watchers were posted to shield the women from unwanted advances. A Winnebago elder has ascribed these practices to "the Hare, the teacher of our customs," who in ancient days was sent by the Winnebago deity Man'una, the Earth Maker, along with four other mythical personages, to rid the world of evil spirits.

By contrast, the Yurok of northwestern California viewed the menstrual seclusion as an escape from mundane chores and a time for

Rasps such as the one above provide musical accompaniment for the Bear Dance, a Ute celebration of a girl's coming of age. To play the instrument, a musician rubs a stick across its teeth. The sound that results resembles the growling of a bear, the animal that, according to legend, taught the Bear Dance to a Ute hunter centuries ago.

Twelve Ute couples perform the Bear Dance in this buckskin painting. Part of a puberty celebration, the dancing reaches such a fever pitch that couples drop to the ground one by one from exhaustion. When the young candidate for adulthood falls with her partner, she is considered a woman.

spiritual training. They called it "moontime" because they believed that the moon caused all of the fertile women in a Yurok household to menstruate simultaneously. If one of the women fell out of synchronization, she sat in the moonlight and asked the moon to put her back into balance. During their seclusion, the women lived together in a domelike hut, bathed in a sacred pond, and spent their time in deep meditation. According to one Yurok woman, the monthly ritual helped them accumulate spiritual energy and taught them that "the earth has her own moontime."

Indian girls experiencing their first menstrual seclusion were commonly assigned strenuous or tedious tasks. The Kaska of the Canadian Rockies had their young women pluck the needles off a spruce bush, one by one, to develop their finger dexterity and make them more skillful sewers. Thompson Indian girls of British Columbia followed an especially rigorous routine of running, digging, and chopping down trees to build up their strength and stamina. Navajo girls ground corn. In addition to the practical benefits, these duties, it was believed, prevented the girls from growing up lazy, just as fasting or eating a restricted diet deterred them

Having prepared tubs of batter for the "alkaan," a sacred corn cake served at a Navajo girl's puberty ceremony, or Kinaalda, a group of Navajo women line a heated pit with cornhusks. The cake will be baked overnight in the pit and then served to guests.

from greediness and selfishness. Indeed, how a girl behaved during her first menstrual seclusion and the celebration that followed was seen as a harbinger of her adult personality. The Navajo, for example, believed that a girl who became grouchy would grow up meanspirited. Laughter was also frowned upon; if a Navajo girl giggled, she could count on developing wrinkles, bad teeth, and a disagreeably loud personality. If she treated small children unkindly, she would be a bad mother.

The Navajo girls' puberty ceremony, called Kinaalda, is a part of the Blessingway, a larger complex of rites with which the Navajo mark all important events in life. Held as soon as possible after a girl's first menses, it lasts four days and nights and features prescribed activities, from special songs and prayers to ritualized dressing and hair combing. All the activities derive from the original Kinaalda, which the Navajo attribute to Changing Woman, daughter of First Man and First Woman, who grew to maturity in four days. On

A Kiowa boy proudly wears his warrior's attire for the camera. Among the Kiowa, boys as young as nine or 10 took part in fights against the enemy. If they performed bravely in battle, they were regarded as men and respected as warriors.

the fourth day, Changing Woman experienced the first Kinaalda at Gobernador Knob, the Navajo Emergence Place, so that "the human race would multiply."

An important element of the ceremony involves molding the girl's body into the perfect form of Changing Woman through a ritual massage much like the one performed by the Navajo's kin, the Mescalero Apache. The Navajo believe that a girl's body is especially soft and pliable at the time of her first menses and thus can be reshaped into a more beautiful form under the skilled hands of a woman of good character and health. A short girl has her limbs stretched so her body will lengthen, while a tall girl is tapped on the head and on the soles of her feet to inhibit further growth. The molding ritual is also thought to shape a girl's disposition, ridding her of disagreeable traits.

The Kinaalda contains several endurance tests, including running, to ensure that the girl will be energetic, supple, and strong in her adult years. Many taboos regulate the running. First, the girl must begin and end at a hogan, the traditional Navajo home. Made of a framework of poles covered by a thick layer of earth, hogans are considered sacred dwellings by the Navajo because the first one was built by the Holy People, the spirits who roamed the earth in the early days. The girl can run as far and as long as she likes, but she must neither fall down nor look back, for to do so brings bad luck. Other young people usually join in the run to share in the girl's blessings, but only prepubescent girls may run ahead of her. During breaks, the girl laboriously grinds corn for the *alkaan,* a round, sweetened cake that is baked and served as an offering to the sun. The final endurance test comes during the last night of the ceremony. Although fatigued from the previous three days' activities, the girl is required to remain awake until dawn, listening to holy men sing sacred hogan songs invoking the blessings of various spiritual guardians on her, her family, and all their belongings. If the girl falls asleep, she breaks the flow of power and diminishes her chances of a prosperous future.

In some cultures, both girls and boys withdrew to secluded sites at puberty, far from their villages, where they fasted and prayed for a dream that would reveal the spirit that would be their guardian for life. Many tribes of the Great Lakes region began preparing their children for the vision quest ordeal when they were as young as seven or eight. The chil-

A favorite site for vision quests among Gros Ventre boys is this sacred circle of rocks near Snake Butte, on the Fort Belknap Indian Reservation in Montana. A boy seeks a message from the spirit world by fasting and praying at the center of the circle. The images that appear to him in the course of his quest will guide him his entire life.

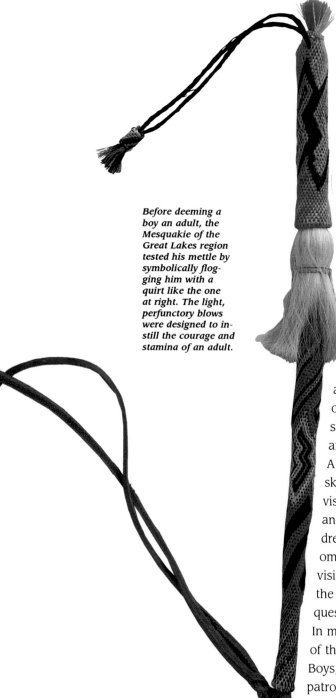

Before deeming a boy an adult, the Mesquakie of the Great Lakes region tested his mettle by symbolically flogging him with a quirt like the one at right. The light, perfunctory blows were designed to instill the courage and stamina of an adult.

dren began with short, practice fasts of only a day, then increased the length of time as they grew older. Although intended to serve as rehearsals for the major vision quests of adolescence, these early experiences sometimes caused children to have powerful dreams, which parents interpreted as preparatory messages from the spirits. Before their first fast, children received their own "fasting sticks," pieces of wood that they partially burned to make ash for blackening their faces—a sign of humility that made the spirits more receptive to their pleas. The more quickly a child used up the fasting stick, the prouder were the parents, for it indicated that he or she was actively seeking communion with the spirits.

The Menominee would send a child off on a major vision quest at about the age of 15. For eight to 10 days, the youngster lived in a tiny wigwam barely large enough to cover him. He fasted and neither saw nor spoke to anyone, except his parents, who visited daily to monitor their child's progress.

If no vision materialized by the eighth day, the parents brought two bowls to the site, one containing charcoal, the other food. The starving and exhausted youth could either accept the food and return home to build up strength for a second try, or blacken his face with the charcoal—a gesture that signaled to the spirits both his sadness at not receiving a vision and his determination to keep on trying.

A fortunate child dreamed of a celestial object or creature of the sky—the sun, moon, stars, or a huge winged spirit bird. Such a vision would enable a boy to become a great hunter or warrior, and a girl to live a long, happy, and virtuous life. Conversely, to dream of the monsters that lived beneath the earth was a bad omen. When Menominee parents heard that their child had been visited by an evil spirit, they would instruct the boy or girl to break the fast immediately. If the dream persisted through two more quests, however, the child's unlucky fate had to be accepted.

In most tribes, girls gave up the vision quest after puberty because of the special power they obtained once they began menstruating. Boys, on the other hand, often continued the effort, for without the patronage of a powerful spirit, a young man could never achieve high status within his community. The importance of a successful vision can be seen in the instructions of a Winnebago father to his son:

This Eskimo mask representing the guillemot features carvings of the bird's wings, feet, and head. It is worn by a dancer at the Bladder Festival, a ceremony held by Alaskan tribes to honor the souls of animals killed during the year and to welcome adolescent boys into the ranks of adult hunters.

"My son, when you grow up, you should try to be of some benefit to your fellow men. There is only one way in which this can be done, and that is to fast. If you thirst yourself to death, the spirits who are in control of wars will bless you. But, my son, if you do not fast repeatedly, it will be in vain that you inflict sufferings upon yourself. Blessings are not obtained except by making the proper offerings to the spirits and by putting yourself, time and again, in the proper mental condition. If you do not obtain a spirit to strengthen you, you will amount to nothing in the estimation of your fellow men, and they will show you little respect."

In some tribes, men continued to fast and seek visions throughout their lives, although the first fast of adolescence was often the most significant, marking the boy's passage into adulthood and determining his social standing within the tribe. Among the Omaha, every adolescent male (and any adolescent female who wanted to) underwent a four-day fasting rite called Nozhizho. The word means "to stand sleeping," a reference to the trance that the youths experienced as they became oblivious to the outside world and conscious only of their own inner selves. If he desired, a boy could repeat the rite every spring until he married, at which time his fate became fixed. During the Nozhizho, the boy went alone to an isolated spot and spread clay over his head to honor the diving animals who, according to Omaha legend, created the earth out of mud from a lake bottom. Then, his mind filled with thoughts of a long and happy life, good health, and success at hunting and war, he

To woo his beloved, a young Apache man played love songs on this fiddle (now missing its strings) made from an agave plant. Music has played a major role in the courtship practices of Native Americans.

prayed to Wakoda, the power that controlled all of nature. Asking for special favors was taboo. With tears streaming down his cheeks, the supplicant stood with hands lifted skyward and sang these words: "Wakoda, the permeating life of nature and of man, / the great mysterious power; / Here, poor, needy, he stands, and I am he. / Wakoda! Here, needy, he stands, and I am he."

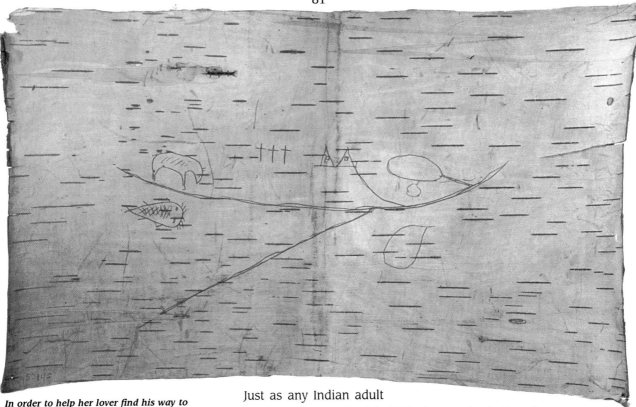

In order to help her lover find his way to her lodge, a young Ojibwa woman scratched this map onto birch bark and slipped it to him during a private moment. Unmarried Ojibwa girls were closely chaperoned by their mothers; a young man might play a flute or fiddle outside a girl's lodge, but she would not be permitted to join him.

Just as any Indian adult would respond to a tearful child, the Omaha believed that Wakoda would have mercy and answer a young man's poignant appeal. The boy then awaited a vision and continued to pray. When the vision came, it usually included a sacred song, which the boy could use throughout his lifetime as a means of summoning help from his guardian spirit in times of crisis. It became his good luck charm as well as his personal connection to the powers of the universe.

The Omaha expected a boy to slip away unobserved to the Nozhizho without asking for counsel. When the youth returned to his lodge, no one questioned him or asked where he had been. For four days, the boy rested, eating and speaking little. Then he sought out an elder who had experienced a similar dream when he was young. After eating and smoking with the elder, the boy set out to find and kill the real-life version of the dream creature that had appeared to him in his vision. He would then take home a piece of it—a hawk's wing or a bear's scalp, for example. This memento became his most sacred possession. Henceforth, whenever he went on the warpath, or took part in a sacred festival or other important event, he either wore it on his body or carried it with him in a medicine bundle.

Dreaming of hawks, elk, and thunder brought good fortune to the Omaha. Visions of snakes portended trouble. But among the Omaha and other tribes, a man who dreamed of the moon courted true disaster, for if he awoke at the wrong moment, he would be forever doomed to give up

his manhood and take up the ways of a woman. Some young men committed suicide after experiencing such dreams. Others accepted their fate and lived the rest of their lives as *mixuga,* which means "instructed by the moon." A mixuga man was obligated to dress like a woman, speak like a woman, and perform the female duties of cultivating the soil, braiding buffalo hair, and embroidering moccasins and clothing. Instead of the warrior's shaved head and decorative roach, the mixuga wore his hair long and parted down the middle.

A few mixuga men crossed back and forth between female and male roles. In 1898 an Osage named Black Dog told a white visitor about a young man who had always insisted that he had received a warrior's vision. After leading a war party on a successful raid, the young man was dancing in honor of his victory when an owl hooted and announced to the Indians that their leader was a mixuga. "The people listened in amazement," Black Dog related, "and the leader protested: 'I have done that which a mixuga could never do!' However, on reaching his home, the young leader dressed as a woman and spoke as a woman. He married and had children. He was successful as a warrior, but when about to go to war, he discarded his woman's clothing and dressed himself as a man."

In other tribes, most notably those of the Great Plains, young men

Wearing colorful headdresses like the one at right, Creek women in Okemah, Oklahoma, perform the Ribbon Dance, an annual ceremony that reaffirms and praises the role of women. Carrying knives to show that they are willing to prepare food for the men, the women proceed solemnly around the public square, stopping once to receive a blessing from the community's chief.

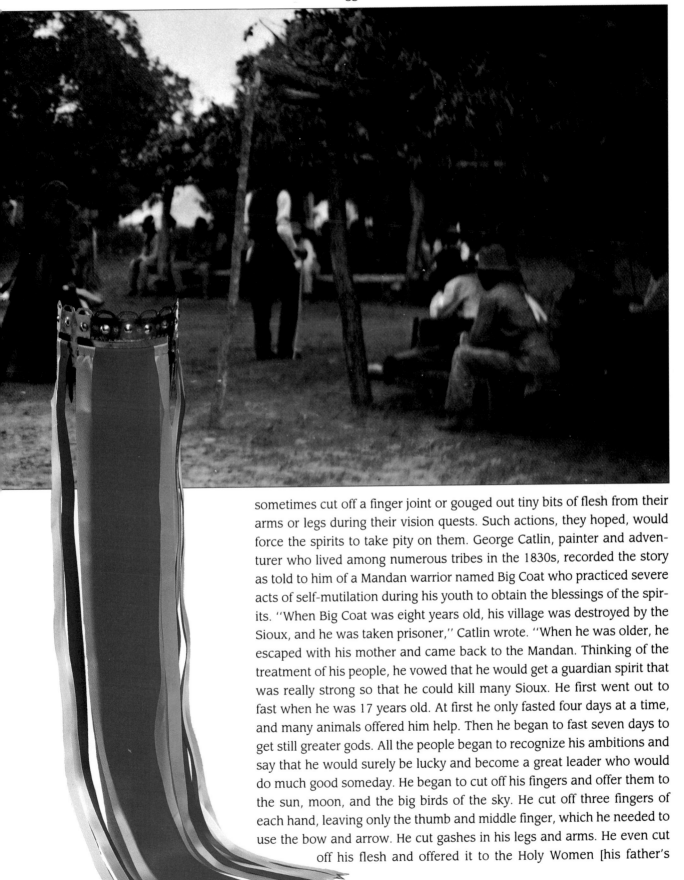

sometimes cut off a finger joint or gouged out tiny bits of flesh from their arms or legs during their vision quests. Such actions, they hoped, would force the spirits to take pity on them. George Catlin, painter and adventurer who lived among numerous tribes in the 1830s, recorded the story as told to him of a Mandan warrior named Big Coat who practiced severe acts of self-mutilation during his youth to obtain the blessings of the spirits. "When Big Coat was eight years old, his village was destroyed by the Sioux, and he was taken prisoner," Catlin wrote. "When he was older, he escaped with his mother and came back to the Mandan. Thinking of the treatment of his people, he vowed that he would get a guardian spirit that was really strong so that he could kill many Sioux. He first went out to fast when he was 17 years old. At first he only fasted four days at a time, and many animals offered him help. Then he began to fast seven days to get still greater gods. All the people began to recognize his ambitions and say that he would surely be lucky and become a great leader who would do much good someday. He began to cut off his fingers and offer them to the sun, moon, and the big birds of the sky. He cut off three fingers of each hand, leaving only the thumb and middle finger, which he needed to use the bow and arrow. He cut gashes in his legs and arms. He even cut off his flesh and offered it to the Holy Women [his father's

Potawatomi men and women once wielded carved effigies, such as the one at left, to cast a love spell on a potential mate. These charms were considered so effective and their power so irresistible that their use was deemed dangerous and akin to coercion.

guardian spirits]. Before he stopped fasting, he had nearly everything as a guardian. He was always successful when leading war parties."

The Luiseno Indians of southern California held an initiation ritual for their young men that lasted several weeks. At the beginning, the boys drank a hallucinogenic drug made from jimson weed and danced until they lapsed into unconsciousness. While insensible, the boys often experienced a guiding vision. Afterward, holy men taught them tribal lore. Part of the instruction consisted of showing the youths a sand painting depicting the various phenomena occupying the Luiseno universe. As the elders explained the meaning of the sand painting, they lectured the boys on proper behavior, concluding with the admonishment: "Heed this speech and you will grow old. And they will say of you, 'He grew old because he heeded what he was told.' And when you die, you will be spoken of as those of the sky, like the stars. Those it is said were people who went to the sky and escaped death. And like those will rise your soul."

Other Native Americans required their young to perform a difficult feat to prove their manhood. The Eskimo boys on Nunivak Island off the west coast of Alaska entered the adult realm by killing a bearded seal—a feat the Nunivak considered the greatest hunting accomplishment next to slaying a polar bear. After returning from the sea with his quarry, the youth went directly to the kashim, the special living and ceremonial quarters for the village males. Before entering with his prize, he sang one of his family's secret hunting songs. The seal's plentiful meat was divided among the elders, while its skin and bladder were hung from the ceiling. There they remained until the village's next Bladder Festival, a celebration held each December to honor all the animals that had surrendered their bodies to feed the Nunivak during the year. The Nunivak believed that an animal's soul resided in its bladder; thus they carefully collected and stored the bladders of the animals they killed until the Bladder Festival, when all the animal souls were returned to the sea.

Between the time of his successful hunt and the annual Bladder Festival, the Nunivak boy had to adhere to a variety of taboos. He could not eat any kind of seal meat, nor could he remove his clothes at night for sleeping. The behavior of his mother was also restricted. Both mother and son had to wear mittens whenever they went outside, even in summer. Both fasted together during the five-day Bladder Festival, which included dancing, singing, and comic speeches. On the final night of the celebration, after the Nunivak had placed all the animal bladders under the ice that covered the sea's surface, the young man stripped naked and ran along the beach. He and his mother then resumed normal living habits. His childhood was officially ended, and he was now eligible to marry.

Indian women generally married men older than they were. The Tlingit, who lived along the Pacific Northwest coast, deemed it a disgrace if a girl did not marry within a few months of her first menses. Most Navajo women also married in the first year following their Kinaalda. Among many other tribes, however, it was the custom to wait until the girls had reached their late teens and developed the skills required of good wives.

The marital age of men varied from tribe to tribe. Some wed in their late teens or early twenties. Others waited until they were older. Arapaho men usually postponed taking on the responsibilities of starting a family until after the age of 30. "In old days, it was customary for a man to marry only after he was quite mature," an Arapaho elder once told a white visitor. "He had to prove that he was a man before he married. He had probably been on the warpath two or three times. Being successful in a war was like passing a character test. He must have had success, too, in hunting and killing buffalo. A girl was ready to be married after her maturity, and after she had been trained by her mother to do the things expected of a woman. She had to be able to tan hides, handle meat, and do the things

To maintain his good looks and popularity among women, a well-groomed Hidatsa bachelor relied on the portable cosmetics kit at right. Inside a decorated buckskin pouch, he carried a hairbrush crafted from porcupine skin and a checkered cloth filled with plant shavings for making face paint.

At a New Year's Eve dance in Pryor, Montana, a Crow pair exuberantly lead a line of couples in the Two-Step, a courting dance that calls for the women to choose their partners. A man who turns down a woman must pay her either with money or with part of his costume.

necessary to run a home. A man was always older than his first wife. I was over 30 when I was married the first time. My first wife was about 19."

For young husbands in matrilineal tribes, such as the Iroquois and the Cherokee, in which descent was traced back through the mother to a common female ancestor, marriage marked a major change in lifestyle. Cherokee villages normally contained only about 350 people, so that most men had to seek wives outside their own community. After the marriage, the new husband was obliged to leave his family and move into his wife's household, which was dominated by his mother-in-law and where he occupied a position inferior to his wife's father and her brothers. It is perhaps not surprising that many young Cherokee warriors spent as much as one-third of their time away from home on extended hunting or trading trips, visiting distant relatives, or as members of war parties.

Usually, families selected their children's marriage partners, although a son's or daughter's wishes might be followed if the parents thought the match a good one. Sometimes the young woman was permitted to reject a suitor who did not appeal to her; if her parents insisted on the marriage, however, she acceded to their demands. To obtain a husband for their daughter, parents looked for a young man from a respected family who had proved himself to be a good hunter and provider. To find a qualified wife for a son, parents sought out a girl of high social standing, solid domestic skills, industrious habits, and a modest demeanor. "Mothers trained their daughters to be good," explained an Arapaho woman. "No good man would want to marry a girl who had no sense. Girls who were especially liked were those who didn't look all around but kept their eyes cast down, and girls who always minded their own business."

Physical attractiveness normally played little part in the choosing of a marriage partner, but an exception could be found among the Makah Indians of the Pacific Northwest, who valued strength in men and beauty in women. To improve her chances of attracting a desirable mate, a Makah girl plucked her eyebrows and began restricting the amount of food she ate as soon as she reached puberty. She rubbed her face and body daily

Dubbed "badé," or "not man, not woman," Crow men like Finds Them and Kills Them (above) preferred the duties and dress of women. Respected for their mastery of female crafts, they sometimes donned male attire and became warriors. Finds Them and Kills Them earned his name in 1876 when he attacked a Lakota war party.

with brushes made of the inner bark fiber of young cedar trees and the tips of fine hemlock branches, a practice believed to keep the skin from sagging. She also sat for hours with her back pressed against the wall of her family's house in order to develop good posture. Young Makah men sought physical perfection by engaging in wrestling and other sports that developed muscles. In addition, they took special night baths during the waxing moon, rubbed their bodies with herbs or bundles of hemlock branches, and prayed to the spirits for greater strength.

An Osage wedding party boards a carriage bound for the groom's home in this 1890s photograph. Their festive attire features U.S. military tunics with gold epaulets and top hats trimmed with ostrich feathers. President Thomas Jefferson introduced these colorful outfits to the tribe as gifts when he honored a visiting Osage delegation. Eventually, these items became traditional Osage wedding wear.

Courtship methods evolved according to tribal custom. Crow warriors often pursued the women they desired by requesting their help on buffalo hunts or during the annual fall expedition into the mountains to cut tipi poles. The young couples worked together during these trips at their appointed male and female tasks, much as they would in marriage. Another popular Crow courtship ritual was the annual berry scramble, when a young man could make known his intentions toward a young woman. Dressed in their best clothes, the young people gathered near a berry patch. Each boy approached the girl of his choice and asked for permission to carry her berry bag. If rebuffed, the young man felt shamed; if accepted, elated. The girls then lined up facing the berry patch and, on a signal, raced to be the first to claim the spot thickest with fruit. The girls broke off several branches and took them to their waiting suitors, who helped pick the berries. The young people then exchanged horses with their chosen partners and paraded back to camp, with each girl riding slightly behind her suitor and joining him in song.

Many men—and sometimes women—resorted to love charms to win the affection of the person they wished to wed. After nightfall, Crow men at times wooed their women by blowing on a long flutelike instrument that imitated the sound of an elk, an animal believed to have strong love powers. Some men also used special medicine bundles—sacred objects acquired as the result of a vision—to cast love spells. Early in the 19th century, a Crow named Travels went into the mountains to fast after being rejected repeatedly by the woman he wished to marry. On the fifth day of the fast, he had a vision in which an elk-man wearing a painted elk-skin robe spoke to him. "When you go home make a robe like that which I am wearing now," the elk-man told him. "Paint it as this one is

painted. Put it on and walk in front of the girl you love. Sing my songs and whistle. She will not refuse you again." Travels did as instructed. He killed a large bull elk and fashioned its skin into a replica of the robe he had seen in his vision. He wore the robe for a single day. The following morning, Travels related, the woman who had spurned him came to his tipi and said she would be his wife.

Cherokee men who were suffering from unrequited love frequently sought the advice of a medicine man, or conjurer, who would prescribe a specific love charm ritual, such as one that involved taking a length of wild grapevine to a stream or river just before sunrise. Facing east, the man would state the name and clan of the woman whose affection he desired, then shred the vine and mix it with a handful of tobacco. With the compound pressed between the palms of his hands, he would raise his arms, thumbs upward, in the direction of the rising sun, and then lower them. Next he would place the mixture in the palm of his left hand and, while singing a love charm song taught to him by the conjurer, roll it in a counterclockwise motion with the four fingers of his right hand. After each line of the song, the man would blow his breath upon the tobacco mixture and spit on it, giving the compound magical powers. Back in the village, he would light the blend four times each day for four days, blowing its smoke in the direction of the girl he desired. It was believed that

if she sniffed the smoke, she would become irresistibly attracted to him.

Among some Plains tribes, such as the Arapaho and the Cheyenne, men often spent several years courting their brides. Because adolescents of opposite sexes were not permitted to openly associate with one another, a youth had to find surreptitious ways of attracting the attention of the girl he wished to wed. He might wait patiently along a path near the girl's home, hoping to encounter her as she went to get water or wood. When the girl finally appeared, the young man would tug gently on her skirt or whistle softly, a sign that he wished to speak with her. The girl could either ignore him, thus rejecting him outright as a suitor, or stop and speak

Flanked by carved cedar poles depicting family crests, a sumptuously attired Kwakiutl bride (center), her father (far left), and other relatives prepare to perform a dance during a reenactment of the wedding ceremony. At Kwakiutl weddings, the families of the bride and groom displayed their wealth and exchanged lavish gifts.

with him. If the conversation went well, other furtive encounters would follow, including discreet meetings held dangerously close to the girl's tipi. One Arapaho man has described a common subterfuge used by the young men. "Tipis always faced east," the Arapaho explained. "On each side of the entrance there was always a pole, the upper end of which was attached to a flap used in controlling the emission of smoke. It might be evening. Two or three persons might be visiting and telling stories in the tipi in which a girl lived. The mother would be sitting by and listening in, too. So would the girl. Both were probably doing some woman's work, liked beading. Now a certain man wanted to see that girl and talk to her. Suppose the wind was blowing from the south or north. The man being on the outside of the tipi would manage to take the poles that were controlling the smoke flaps and move them so as to cause the smoke to blow into the tipi. The father of the girl would then say, 'There is smoke in here. The wind must have changed. Go, change the poles.' So the girl goes out to change the poles and notices that the wind hasn't changed, but that there is a man out there who wants a chance to talk to her."

When a young man felt sure enough about his choice for a wife, he would ask his relatives for their assistance in approaching the girl's family. If they approved of the match, his relatives would assemble a collection of valuable items—blankets, clothing, bows and arrows, horses—and

At Fort Rupert, British Columbia, in 1915, a stack of box lids awaits delivery to a bridegroom (below, right). Such lids once covered wooden boxes used to carry gifts from the bride's home to the groom's; they eventually became symbols of wealth in their own right. Another emblem of prosperity was the dowry board (below, left), presented personally to the groom by his bride.

send them, along with a respected emissary from the family, to the parents of the bride-to-be. After some friendly tobacco smoking and small talk, the emissary would present the gifts and the proposal to the girl's parents, then leave before receiving an answer. The young woman's male relatives would then convene in the father's tipi for a discussion of the pros and cons of the proposed marriage. If they rejected the offer, the family returned the gifts. If they accepted, they distributed the gifts among themselves. They then dressed the girl in her best buckskin outfit, amassed gifts of equal value to those given by the boy's family, and sent both the girl and gifts, accompanied by her mother and another woman, to the home of her husband-to-be. A marriage feast followed.

In Blackfeet communities, it was the family of the girl, not that of the boy, who made the initial offer of marriage. "When a girl's parents decided upon a son-in-law, the father made the proposal by saying that his daughter would carry food to the young man's lodge," noted Walter McClintock, an amateur anthropologist who lived among the Blackfeet people around the end of the 19th century. "If he was favourable, she carried food to him daily for a moon. Everyone would know of the girl's actions, and the engagement would be talked of throughout the camp." Once a girl became engaged, her father, rather than her mother or another female relative, had the responsibility of instructing her about what would be expected of her as a married woman.

The parents of the bride-to-be had to provide each of their daughter's

Crafted from sedge root and willow, and covered with red-headed woodpecker, mallard, quail, and meadowlark feathers, baskets like the ones above were treasured wedding gifts among the Pomo of California. Gathering the rare feathers could take months or years, and weaving them onto the surface of a basket called for the skills of a master artist.

The twin spouts of this jug from Acoma Pueblo in New Mexico symbolize the union of marriage. During the wedding ceremony, the bride drinks from one spout, the groom from the other.

future in-laws with a pair of moccasins decorated with porcupine quills. These were delivered at the wedding feast, which was arranged by the girl's family, but held at the boy's home. "When everything was in readiness, the mother and daughter carried the food and moccasins to his lodge," explained McClintock. "The girl then entered alone. Without a word being spoken, she took her seat on the boy's right and distributed the moccasins and food. During the feast, her mother remained outside. It was not proper for her to enter the lodge of her future son-in-law. After the feast, the man gave to his prospective wife many presents, bidding her to distribute them among her relatives, who had given presents to his family." With this exchange of gifts, the young couple went off to live in a new tipi, prepared and furnished by the girl's mother.

Sometimes a girl refused to marry the man selected for her by her family because she had another sweetheart. When this occurred among the Tlingit, the parents of the girl might allow her true love to work for them for years, killing deer, providing fish, and chopping wood, until at last they gave their daughter permission to marry him. Some couples, fearing opposition to their marriage by either or both sets of their parents, cohabited in secret. Among the Osage, this course of action had serious consequences, particularly for the man, who would lose status should the secret be discovered. He could never become a *nigka-donhe,* or "good man," a title of honor bestowed upon elderly Osage men when they became grandfathers. This was because the Osage did not consider the children of such unions to be legitimate people.

Although most cultures frowned on unsanctioned marriages, not all discounted them so harshly. The Arapaho accepted such "sweetheart marriages," as they called them, albeit begrudgingly. If a woman wished to elope with a man, she simply arranged to meet him secretly by night, and they rode off together to live among his family. "There will be no ceremonial in this case, but the tribe accepts the couple as being married," the Arapaho said. "There may be ill feeling for some

*A Mesquakie wom-
an used the bone
needle at right, the
first present from
her new husband, to
weave a sacred
grass prayer mat
(left) for their home.
Such mats were
usually the first
household item a
new bride created.*

time, but after the blow is over, which may take six months or a year, things continue on very well."

In many communities, men customarily took more than one wife. In several Plains tribes, when a man married the oldest sister in a family, he was also entitled to marry the younger ones as they came of age. Such marriages were considered eminently practical: They usually required no ceremony, for the two families were already considered bonded. The man simply gave his father-in-law a horse or other gift, and then the younger sister moved into his home. This custom allowed families to avoid many of the inheritance problems involved in having several sons-in-law. Many wives also welcomed the arrangement, for it meant a lighter work load and the companionship of women with whom they were less likely to quarrel. But not all wives relished the thought of sharing a husband and a home with their sisters. Decades after the event, an Arapaho woman still spoke angrily of her family's decision to marry her to her brother-in-law. "When I was 15, my parents decided that I was to marry," she recalled. "The man to whom they wanted me to be married was then 30 and already married to my oldest sister. Just because my sister was married to him was no reason why I should be. I did not wish to marry this man, but my parents asked my brother if he was satisfied. He was, and so I had to get married to him." Other women were not so compliant, however, and resorted to eloping with a lover to escape marriage to an in-law.

When a man had two or more wives who were not related, he often established separate houses for each one in order to promote harmony and provide adequate living space. The first wife, however, usually supervised the work of all the subsequent wives and retained special privileges of rank. The Blackfeet called a man's first wife his "sits beside him wife" because she always sat on her husband's right—the position of honor—during family gatherings and ceremonies. In a few, very rare instances, it was the woman who took on a second spouse, in which case she looked after two separate homes. A man of the Washo tribe in the region around Nevada told of a woman in his village who had married two brothers many years earlier. "They got along fine," he recalled. "She rustled food for both of them. She had one girl and two boys by one man and no children by the other. They didn't live together. They had two *galis dangal* [winter houses] along the West Carson River."

Some communities permitted the exchanging of spouses. The Netsil-ik Inuit called this practice *kipuktu* and engaged in it frequently. The hus-

Wedding baskets like the ones above feature concentric rings symbolic of rain and fertility. Breaking across these rings is a line stretching from the center of the basket to its perimeter, making a pathway that permits the spirits within the basket to emerge.

For generations, the Navajo of Arizona and New Mexico relied on baskets for everything from carrying water to storing nuts and seeds. Although these sturdy receptacles bore the demands of daily domestic life well, they have been largely abandoned in favor of more durable and convenient containers made from modern materials. A traditional Navajo marriage ceremony, however, still calls for a wedding basket especially woven and decorated for the occasion.

Used to hold sacred cornmeal mush for the bride and groom and their guests, a wedding basket is usually one foot or more in diameter and three to four inches deep. During the nuptials, the bride's father sprinkles two lines of pollen across the mush, the first stretching from east to west, the second from south to north. The bride and groom eat from the east, south, west, north, and center of the basket and then share the food with their guests. Whoever eats the last bit of mush keeps the basket; the recipient may not put the basket to any mundane use but is allowed to display it at home in a place of honor.

The Navajo women who once wove most of the tribe's baskets, including wedding baskets, observed a number of taboos. They did not work while menstruating, for example, and underwent ritual cleansing before and after making a basket. Constraints like these proved so tedious and time-consuming that the Navajo ended up hiring Ute and Paiute women to do the work.

Bundles of split sumac branches and yucca leaves are the materials used for the coils that form a wedding basket. The yucca leaves are twisted to make the coils; the coils are sewn together with the sumac strips. The red and black designs on older baskets were created from plant and mineral dyes.

Two Navajo women weave wedding baskets in front of their hogan near Kayenta, Arizona. Although trade goods such as metal cups and plates caused a decline in basket making during the 1880s, the demand for ceremonial baskets has risen in modern times.

Long, cylindrical shells of the mollusk dentalium have been combined with Chinese coins and glass beads to form a stunning bridal headdress (left). Brides among the Wishram Indians in Canada (right) wore these as symbols of their family's wealth and prestige.

band usually initiated the transaction, exchanging his wife for the wife of a good friend. Kipuktu reinforced the deep bond of friendship between the two men, who often were also partners in certain rituals. Some of these arrangements lasted for only a brief time—a man might borrow a friend's wife for a long trip, for example—but others continued on and off for many years. Not all exchanges ended well. Many resulted in bitter jealousies and ruined both the marriages and the friendships. The Crow permitted *batsuera-u,* or "wife stealing," but only between members of two rival warrior societies, the Kit Foxes and the Lumpwoods. For a brief period every spring, members of these prestigious groups could slip into each other's dwellings and abduct each other's wives.

Unsanctioned infidelity could bring harsh punishment, particularly for women. When a Crow woman committed adultery, her husband might beat her or slash her face with a knife. Unfaithful Blackfeet and Arapaho women suffered greater punishments. If a husband even suspected his wife of having a lover, he had the right to cut off her nose or earlobe, or even to kill her. "I had a grandmother, my mother's mother, whose husband was jealous of her and cut her nose off with a knife," said one Arapaho woman. "She was ashamed of her nose after that and would hold her hand before her face when talking to people." Sometimes a betrayed husband simply threw the offending wife out of the house. "My younger brother had two sisters for his wives," recalled an Arapaho man. "The people kept telling him that one was unfaithful. But he wouldn't believe what he heard. He said, 'I have to see her doing this with my own eyes before I believe it.' But he saw her. He happened to see her going into a tipi. So he went there, and he found her with the man all right. He brought her back to his tipi. He made her dress up in her best clothes and fix up her hair. Then he gave her his

In this photograph taken about 1880, a Sioux warrior sits proudly with his two wives. Polygamy was once an accepted form of marriage among many Indian tribes, although generally only wealthy men could afford to support more than one wife.

best horse, put her on the horse, and took her over to this man to whom she had been talking and said, 'Here, you can have her!' ''

A husband also had the right to take revenge on his wife's lover. Once, a Tlingit man killed his sister's son after discovering the younger man coming out of a secret opening to his wife's bedroom. He cut off the young man's head and hung it over the doorway of his house, a drastic act that triggered a family feud that lasted for decades. Among the Mandan and the Hidatsa, when a married woman ran off with another man, her husband could avenge his honor by killing the horses of the man's brothers and sisters, who were held accountable for his behavior. If the husband held a prestigious position in the community, he might organize a war party to track down the runaway couple and reclaim his wife, even if it meant risking open warfare with the other man's relatives. Few men did so, however, for to brood over a lost wife or attempt to get her back was considered bad form and caused most men to lose status within their communities. Such was the case with Four Bears, a Hidatsa war chief whose wife was stolen by a Mandan warrior named Bear on the Water. After the couple eloped, the angry Four Bears refused to be appeased by Bear on the Water's relatives, who offered to compensate him with horses for his loss. Instead, Four Bears demanded the return of his wife, saying she was needed at his home to tend to her ill child, although everyone in his village knew that he had other wives who could care for the child. When he began making

To punish her for infidelity, the husband of this Apache woman sliced off the tip of her nose, rendering her undesirable to other men. Punishment by physical disfigurement was common among many tribes, although some men and women divorced an unfaithful mate by simply setting his or her belongings outside their dwelling.

threats against Bear on the Water's family, they felt compelled to leave their village to avoid a blood feud. It was Four Bears, however, who drew the disdain of the village for behavior deemed unworthy of a chief.

Once married, couples had to adhere to strict rules governing their relationships with their in-laws and other family members. Tribal custom dictated that they could be familiar with some relatives but not with others. Among the Blackfeet, for example, a man was forbidden to speak to his mother-in-law; nor could she speak to him. If a woman wished to visit her married daughter, she did so in her son-in-law's absence. Some Plains Indians believed this practice reduced quarreling and contributed to the general well-being of the community. It was also viewed as a sign of respect. In Blackfeet villages, a man could not even be seen in the presence of his wife's mother, whether they spoke or not. If a man broke this taboo—even unintentionally—he would have to make amends to his mother-in-law by giving her a horse.

In Cheyenne communities, a special exchange of gifts could override the taboo between mother-in-law and son-in-law. A man began the process by honoring his mother-in-law with the gift of a horse he had captured in battle. The gift, of course, was always presented through a third person. The mother-in-law returned the honor by giving her son-in-law a valuable article of her own making. If she was a member of the Robe Quillers Society, for example, she might make him a fine buffalo robe embroidered in dyed porcupine quills. Once the robe was finished, the mother-in-law held a feast for the Quillers Society in her home. The son-in-law would be notified about the feast, but when he arrived, he would not enter the tipi; instead, he would simply take the robe, which his mother-in-law would have placed on a horse staked nearby. The horse, too, was a gift for him. From that day on, the mother-in-law–son-in-law taboo was set aside for them. Not every family, however, could attain this privilege—only those with a son-in-law and a mother-in-law who had both achieved high standing within the community.

Among the Nunivak people, a man could not talk to or look directly at either of his parents-in-law. If he and his father-in-law met on a trail outside their village, each would keep his gaze on the ground as they passed. A woman had to follow similar rules regarding her parents-in-law, al-

though the restraints were not as strictly observed as her husband's. A Nunivak wife could speak to her mother-in-law, for example, as long as she refrained from looking at her directly.

As late as the 1930s, anthropologist Sister Inez Hilger visited Arapaho families who still followed the in-law taboo. "In a three-room house of a Southern Arapaho, we found a daughter-in-law sitting alone on the back porch of her house while her 80-year-old father-in-law, who was blind, sat on his bed in a front room of the same house," Hilger reported. "The woman's husband and her children had gone to town to a baseball game. She had spent the entire afternoon alone, and so had her father-in-law."

Hilger asked the daughter-in-law about the taboo. "If I would talk to him, he would think that I had no respect for him," she explained. "That's what the old people all say. I wouldn't talk to him unless it was really necessary. For instance, if he took sick suddenly and there was no one else around here, then I would have to talk to him. Having to sit alone like this and not being allowed to talk to my father-in-law is really hard. He is a good man, and I have always admired him. He is lonely now, too, because he does not know where his son is, the one in the army."

Such taboos did not extend to certain other in-law relationships, however. Young men usually enjoyed a familiar relationship with their sisters-in-law, although one marked by horseplay and practical jokes played on both sexes. "It was the practice to dash cold water on one's

Arvol Looking Horse and Carol Ann Heart (left) bask in the joy of being husband and wife after their wedding on the Cheyenne River Indian Reservation in South Dakota. Before the ceremony, Looking Horse and several guests watch as two eagles circle overhead (below). The eagle is sacred to the Lakota Sioux, and the presence of two at the wedding augured well for the marriage.

brother-in-law if he was caught asleep, and vice versa, no matter how cold the weather, which was a great joke,'' recalled an elderly Arapaho woman in 1932. ''I always got up very early in the morning, so that joke was never played on me.'' Another favorite prank was to sneak into such in-laws' tipis while they slept and blacken their noses and eyebrows with soot from a cooking kettle.

For the Seminole, joking between a man and his sisters-in-law was not only permitted but openly encouraged. When it came time to choose team leaders for a favorite Seminole ball game that pitted a group of

women against a group of men, the teams usually selected a young man and his sister-in-law. The players knew that the relationship between these two allowed bodily contact and that they would not refrain from playing hard, even if it meant tearing each other's clothes off. Seminole men had similar joking, or *cahacawa,* relationships with other relatives, but none of these was as intense or as intimate as the joking relationship with their wives' sisters, who were, after all, potential future spouses.

Some tribes, such as the Cherokee, permitted friendly relations between adult brothers and sisters, but most Indians required that siblings of opposite sexes avoid direct contact after puberty to help enforce the universal taboo against incest. "After they are 10 years old, or even before, we don't like sisters and brothers to play together or to wrestle," explained one Jicarilla Apache. "A boy can't drink from the same cup from which his sister has drunk or eat the bread from which she has taken a bite. A boy can't say anything dirty in front of his sister, and he can't come into a tipi where his sister is alone. Someone else might think he was 'staying with his sister' and might talk against him."

The same sort of restrictions extended in some tribes to boy and girl first cousins—depending on who their parents were. The children of siblings of the same sex—two brothers or two sisters—were by custom members of the same clan and were governed by clan sexual taboos. These cousins abided by all the rules of sibling relationships and were referred to as brothers and sisters. Marriage between them was forbidden because it would constitute incest. First cousins descended from siblings of opposite sexes, however, were traditionally members of different clans and were governed by more lenient rules. In some tribes, they might be allowed to marry. But in other communities, restraint was exercised among first cousins no matter what their parentage. "My father's sister had a daughter," recalled an older Apache man. "To a girl related to you in this way you don't pass anything. You put it down, and she comes and gets it. You don't touch her; you don't come close to her; you don't touch her dress or even her moccasins. But I used to hide from this girl altogether. I was bashful with her, just as a man is with his mother-in-law. I didn't go near her. I wasn't exactly afraid; I was just sort of ashamed. No one in particular started the hiding. We both did it and kept away from each other. Not all hide like this, but all are careful with their cousins."

Divorce was a simple matter in most tribes. Usually all that was required was for the spouse to move out of the home. Sometimes husbands threw

A Stoney Indian couple of Alberta, dressed in their finest outfits, sit with their young son for a family portrait, taken in 1907. Despite the fact that most tribes have adapted to Western ways, traditional beliefs about courtship and marriage still form the bedrock of numerous Indian communities.

their wives out; other times, the women left on their own. Crow men sometimes divorced their wives for being quarrelsome or cranky. Small children of divorced couples always went to live with their mothers, although when the boys became older, they were reclaimed by the fathers. The Crow had a custom of publicly "throwing away" an unwanted wife or husband during a festivity known as the Hot Dance. During the dancing, a special song was sung, at which time those wishing to rid themselves of their spouse could announce their intentions. The Arapaho had a similar tradition. "A man would go to the drummers, beat the drum with a stick, throw the stick away, and say, 'Whoever wants my wife may have her, and her tipi and some horses, too,' " an Arapaho man said. Any man who picked up the stick became the woman's new husband.

Such simple rituals made the process of divorce for Native Americans look easy, but in reality, as in all cultures, separation from a partner could be emotionally devastating and produce lasting scars. Maria Chona, a Papago woman, arrived home one day in the mid-1800s to find her husband's second wife sitting under the arbor outside her house. Her husband, a young medicine man, had married again without telling her. Chona found this unacceptable, and she left rather than share him with another woman. Some 70 years later, Chona told a white visitor about the events that followed. The memory still caused her sadness.

"I piled my clothes in a basket, and I put in a large butcher knife," Chona recalled. "I thought if he followed, I would kill him. Then I took my little girl and went away." Chona walked all that day and the next to the house of her brother, who quickly arranged for her to marry another man—an old, rich widower with many horses. Chona still hoped that her first husband would come for her and send his second wife away. But her brother insisted that she regain her honor and marry the older man.

"I did not say anything," Chona recalled. "No woman has a right to speak against her brother. But I felt bad. I did not love that old man. I used to go in the washes and lie flat under the greasewood bushes and cry. Or I would lie on the floor in the house when my husband was away, covered up with blankets. It hurt." Chona never saw her first husband again. She later learned that he had been deserted within months by his second wife, and that the following spring he had gotten sick and died. As he lay dying, he had called out for her many times. "His brother came to tell me. I cried," Chona said. "I used to go behind a hill, away from the house, and cry half the day. He almost took me with him. I kept thinking at night that the door would open and he would take me by the hand. I would cry out. My new husband said, 'What is wrong? You always cry.' I told him, 'He comes and pulls me up.' Next day, my husband said nothing. He got on a horse and rode far off there to the grave. He said, 'Leave her alone. It's your own fault. If you come for her again, I'll dig you up and burn your bones.' After that, the dead was quiet."

For every marriage that ended in grief, however, there were many others that survived life's vicissitudes and remained solid through the years. Many unions flourished as a couple's affection and respect for each other intensified over time. So it was with the marriage of Powder Face, an Arapaho chief. A white man who visited the home of Powder Face in 1883 gave the following description of the old warrior and his wife: "He did not rise, but continued his ministrations to his wife as he bade me be seated," the visitor recalled. "The two had been married many years and had no children. Powder Face had never taken another wife, and this one was his willing slave to the day of his death. He helped her with many duties commonly falling to the lot of the women and was a lover always. On this first meeting with the couple, he did not seem to mind me and continued to stroke her hair into place as he spoke words of endearment. He oiled her hair and braided it for her."

*Astride a feather-bedecked horse, a stylishly attired Lakota
warrior approaches a young woman in this late-19th-century drawing;
both carry umbrellas, a Plains fashion of the period. Male suitors dressed as they
would when going to meet the spirits, donning their finest clothes and
carefully grooming their hair so as to appear fresh and pure.*

COURTSHIP ON THE PLAINS

"In the old days, it was not so very easy to get a girl when you wanted to be married," Black Elk, Oglala Sioux medicine man, once commented. "Sometimes it was hard work for a young man, and he had to stand a great deal." Among the Sioux and other Plains tribes, both sexes had to earn the right to marry—men by proving themselves as hunters and warriors, women by demonstrating their mastery of crafts and farming skills. Courtship began with the attempts of a young man to secure a girl's affection, usually through quiet conversation in public. To augment their powers of persuasion, suitors invoked supernatural aid, consulting shamans and other amatory specialists who supplied medicine that would ensure success in love.

When a young man felt confident of a favorable reception, he enlisted his brother or a close friend to extend a formal proposal to his intended's male relatives. A girl could veto any man she deemed unappealing. But if she found her suitor acceptable, the intermediaries proceeded with the details. Negotiations typically involved agreeing on a bride price—as generous a gift in horses, food, and other goods as the groom could afford. In no way seen as direct payment for a wife, such gifts demonstrated a man's potential as a provider and acknowledged the woman's value to her family.

Some couples, impatient with these formalities, dispensed with them and simply ran off together, an alternative usually accepted as a de facto marriage. But unions forged through formal, community-sanctioned courtship were more favorably regarded in close-knit Sioux society, affirming that the act of establishing a family was honored as a crucial part of Plains life.

Favorite flute motifs included the woodpecker, thought to have created the first flute by pecking hollow branches; the crane, whose long neck was seen as an erotic symbol; and the prairie chicken, noted for its showy courtship.

THE MAGIC OF MUSIC

The timeless allure of music was an indispensable element of Sioux courtship. Men serenaded young women with courting flutes, slender flageolets crafted by shamans who often carved them into effigies of animals associated with love and sexual passion. Each flute was accompanied by magical love music composed by the shaman according to instructions received from a dream.

A suitor played the flute in order to attract a girl's attention and to let her know that he wanted to talk to her. According to a Lakota named Leader Charge, "Some flutes were so powerful that a girl, hearing the melody, would become so nervous that she would leave her tipi and follow the sound. Many flutes had such power that if a man should touch a woman with it, she became so entranced that she would go with her lover anywhere."

The Lakota chief White Swan, depicted in beadwork on a hide tipi bag, regales a woman with tales of his battlefield exploits. Reciting war honors was an established rite of courtship.

A HOPI WEDDING

Among the Hop[...]
traditional wed[...]
union of a mar[...]
cerem[...]
sage[...]
and c[...]
community and the kach[...]
that regulate the lives of t[...]
duty of nurturing new life[...]
her life, she will be deem[...]
enter the spirit world only[...]
tions as a wife and mothe[...]
bound to reward her dedi[...]
upon her community and h[...]

In modern times, man[...]
church or civil ceremonies[...]

A radiant bride contemplates her upcoming wedding while the groom's mother arranges her hair into two loose coils, the usual style for married Hopi women.

On the wedding day, the daughter of the bride and groom is dusted with sacred cornmeal. Hopi couples often have children by the time they can organize the elaborate traditional wedding.

The groom's mother sits patiently while a relative styles her hair for the wedding (right). Before any sacred occasion, men and women alike pay special attention to their hair, washing it with soap made from the root of the yucca plant.

The groom's father wraps ears of corn, the wedding sash, and the smaller of the two wedding robes in a reed mat that the bride will carry to her family's home (above). On the occasion of her death, the bride will be bundled in the smaller robe for her trip to the spirit world. The corn will nourish her there.

Wearing the larger of her wedding robes, the solemn bride reverently holds her reed case during the final, brief prayer service in the groom's house. Her daughter stands beside her in a similar robe that was woven by the groom's uncles.

*While his fath[...]
groom's kinsme[...]
bride. In exchange[...]
the bride mov[...]
family and spend[...]
grinding corn,[...]*

After the wedding, the bride leads a procession to her parents' house; behind her, the groom carries a side of mutton, and his relatives bring food and gifts for his new wife. When the bride is received by her mother, the wedding rites will be over and the feasting will begin. The couple will live with the bride's family until they can build their own house.

Tassels dangling from the bride's wedding robe in its reed case represent fertility. They were blessed during the wedding ceremony in the hope that the couple would have many children.

3

CLOSING THE CIRCLE

Having donned their finest garments and jewelry, an elderly Navajo couple pose before a pile of melons at their village. Because of the spiritual values they embody and the wisdom they have gained through years of living, elders have traditionally been held in the highest esteem by Native Americans.

Like human beings everywhere, Native Americans have aspired to a long and successful life—but with a difference. An Indian's primary responsibility was to the group, not the self. Despite a remarkable diversity of ways of life that evolved in a variety of environments, spanning the continent from the parched American Southwest to the ice and snow of the Canadian Arctic, all Indian peoples placed the welfare of their community first. Whether organized on the basis of mobile bands, clans, or systems of villages, individual Indians saw themselves not as alone or separate but as part of an interconnected whole, embodied by the tribe. And the values and beliefs of the tribe, rooted in legend and passed down through oral tradition, remained forever paramount.

Although different cultures emphasized different values, Indian peoples everywhere saw life as dependent on connections with a vast range of powerful spirits that were associated with all aspects of the physical world. And they sought good health and longevity by observing common rituals inherited by the community. The Tlingit, for example, who fished and hunted on the coast of northern British Columbia and southern Alaska, equated well-being with the notion of physical solidity. Ever since Raven, the Tlingit creator, transformed the world's original human population into rocks and made a new race out of a leaf—and thus made it subject to decay and death—the Tlingit have sought longevity and good fortune by ritually making their bodies more rocklike. They accorded young people the status of adulthood only when the soft cartilage in their joints was no longer discernible—a condition most Tlingit males reached in their midtwenties—and, to pay a compliment, they used the expression, "I make you heavier than anyone." Throughout their adult lives, the Tlingit periodically fasted, drank salt water, bathed in the cold ocean, abstained from sexual relations, and scraped their skin with special stones—ritual actions designed to make their bodies harder and heavier. Wealthy Tlingits amassed ponderous amulets and plates, dressed in bulky robes of marten and sea otter, and wore heavy nose rings, earrings, and bracelets to provide themselves with even more symbolic weight.

Almost universally in Indian communities, leadership was a function

Shortly after receiving a doctoral degree, scholar Ken Pepion, a member of the Blackfeet tribe, is granted an Indian name by his elderly uncle. Older Indians have traditionally been given the honor of bestowing a new name upon an individual to mark a milestone in his life.

of age. The majority of the civil chiefs and leaders of various tribal institutions were experienced elders. Knowing the value of each life to a small community and concerned with the greater good of everyone, the elders frequently counseled restraint when the young warriors wanted to rush off to the warpath. Indian elders also served as the primary providers of childcare and instruction—an ethic that endowed many tribes with the moral strength and resiliency to survive into the present, despite almost overwhelming political, economic, and religious pressures to "walk the white man's road." As a Seminole Indian who was forcibly transplanted to Oklahoma once eloquently said of his tribal elders, "The old people were like the shade of a tree, sheltering the young from the sun."

Nothing shaped the life of an adult Indian more than kinship—the framework that defined how people were related. It was the foundation of social organization. The complexity of kinship systems varied, but in all cases it defined the status, rights, and duties of the members of a specific group. Common blood was not the only means of establishing kinship ties. Many tribes adopted war captives and other outsiders. Kinship systems not only dictated whom a person might marry but also determined such matters as the makeup of households or firesides, and the right to perform certain ceremonies, cultivate certain fields, fish certain waters, or hunt certain hunting grounds. Depending on the tribe, a family's pedigree might be traced through the mother, the father, or both parents.

The Mandan and the Hidatsa, for example, were tribes who traced descent through the female line. After marriage, a woman and her husband shared a lodge with several families that were related through the wife. The women of the lodge tilled garden plots together, distributing the harvest as needed. Although the plots were controlled by the household, the land was considered to belong to a lineage, a larger kinship group consisting of a number of extended families linked through female ances-

At Sitka, Alaska, in December 1904, Tlingit villagers from Yakutat proudly wear the regalia of their Raven Clan. The positions of highest status within the clan were generally held by the elderly, who were more likely to possess the wealth, integrity, and sound judgment required of the leadership in such organizations.

try; individual families in the lineage were assigned as much land as their women could effectively cultivate. Mandan and Hidatsa lineages, in turn, fitted within clans, which claimed common descent from a mythical ancestor through the female line. All members of the tribe were assigned at birth to their mother's clan; mature members were expected to provide aid and protection to others in the clan. If a family fell on hard times, the clan would look after it; if an offense was committed against an individual, the clan could exact revenge. Similarly, if a member of the clan was involved in a crime, the entire clan might be held responsible.

Marriage within clans was forbidden, but a man did not lose contact with his own clan when he married, even though often he moved into his wife's household. He was expected to provide certain types of instruction to the children of his sisters, just as his wife's brothers were expected to teach his own children. He might eventually become a leader of his clan—but of course he could never join his wife's. Language reflected the complex kinship system. A Mandan called his father's relatives the equivalent of "male of my father's mother-line" or "female of my father's mother-line," while using distinctive separate terms for all of his mother's relatives.

Throughout the Indian world, a strict division of labor between the sexes prevailed. Men crafted the weapons and did almost all of the hunting, although women sometimes killed birds and small animals and often helped butcher and carry home the larger game. In the Southwest, men also did most of the farming, but in the East and on the prairies, farming was women's work—although the men might lend a hand in clearing fields and bringing in the harvest. Everywhere women processed and cooked the food, fetched fuel and water, and prepared clothing and other domestic articles. When labor demands were at a maximum—as during a

Combining word and gesture, an experienced Eskimo hunter relates an adventure to a group of children gathered in a tent at a summer fishing camp. He first describes spotting his quarry, probably a walrus or other sea mammal (top left). After paddling his canoe within range, he takes aim with a rifle (top) and fires. Using a straw for tusks, he pretends he is the dead animal and points to the fatal bullet wound (above). Tales such as these not only entertained the children but also served to teach them the skills they would need as adults.

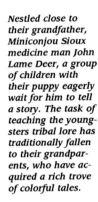

Nestled close to their grandfather, Miniconjou Sioux medicine man John Lame Deer, a group of children with their puppy eagerly wait for him to tell a story. The task of teaching the young-sters tribal lore has traditionally fallen to their grandpar-ents, who have ac-quired a rich trove of colorful tales.

buffalo hunt or at the times of planting and harvesting—men and women joined forces to get the work done, but such occasions were the exception. Usually, the sexes kept to their own spheres, even in such tasks as decoration: Among the Plains Indians, for example, the job of painting pictorial designs on tipis, war shields, and buffalo robes was always performed by men, whereas the women were limited to geometric designs. Women did all of the hide preparation, quilling, and beadwork, however.

The pace of daily life varied according to tribal custom and the constraints of the environment. With the Klamath of the Northwest, for example, the accumulation of possessions—shells, skins, weapons, food—was much encouraged, and anyone who did not strive to build up a store of property was regarded as lazy and held in low esteem. Among the Pueblo peoples, personal wealth lacked such importance, but the challenges of the arid environment fostered a strong work ethic—whether outside in the sprawling fields or inside the dim adobe rooms where each day women ground a fresh batch of cornmeal to feed their families. By contrast, the Mohave Indians, who lived by farming and fishing in the lower Colorado River valley, worked only when the need arose. When something had to be done, they responded with a burst of energy, but they spent much of the time in less strenuous pursuits: visiting friends, telling stories, gambling, and playing a variety of games.

All across the Indian world, most people were competent in a wide range of tasks appropriate to their gender. Nevertheless, certain individuals developed such expertise in particular jobs that others paid them for their work—although such payments rarely accounted for their entire livelihood. In the Pacific Northwest, for example, some men specialized

A Quileute craftsman teaches his young grandson the fine points of canoe building. Although modern Quileutes use planes and motorboats to travel between their communities along the coast of Washington State, canoe building is still a cherished craft passed on from one generation to the next.

Acclaimed Makah carver Frank Allabush displays works in progress in this late-19th-century photograph. The concept of retirement was foreign to Allabush, who began carving dolls as a young man and continued his work until his death.

in canoe making, while others were experts at weaving nets, growing tobacco, or chipping obsidian. Men with physical ailments that prevented active work toiled at sedentary tasks requiring great patience and manual dexterity, such as rubbing elk horn into spoons or gluing feathers for ceremonial regalia. Similarly, a woman might be recognized as exceptionally gifted at basket making or some other female pursuit. Occupational skill was viewed not just as a matter of natural talent or long practice; like exceptional ability in hunting or war, it was seen as a gift from the spirits.

Among the Mandan of the Missouri River prairies, some men were especially skilled arrow makers, singers, or storytellers. Some women were admired for their ability to make pottery or paint designs on animal skins. Such specialized know-how was considered to be a personal possession and had great value;

Still active although nearly 100 years old, a Yurok woman nimbly weaves a storage basket in this photograph that was taken in the early 20th century. Her finished product will represent a lifetime of acquired skills.

Flanked by his two wives, a Tlingit medicine man sits proudly for a family portrait. Although an effective medicine man was well honored for his work, it could still take years for him to earn enough prestige to attract a second wife.

Because older medicine men, such as the Assiniboin healer below, drew upon a lifetime of experience, their cures were often considered more potent than those of younger healers.

communal ceremonies held at important times of the year to beseech the gods—when crops were planted, when the salmon began to run, when the summer rains were due, when war or hunting parties set out. Through all these ritual observances, great and small, life was infused with spirituality.

Contact with the spirit world was achieved not only through rituals and visions but also by way of nighttime dreams. Everywhere in Indian America, dreams were thought to provide access to the realm of spirits, and people paid close attention to their contents, believing that a dream could reveal important truths. Some dreams foretold the future, although perhaps obliquely. The Tlingit, for example, believed that a dream about catching a fish might portend the catching of a valuable animal in a trap, or a dream of eating seaweed might augur death, since the eating of "beach food" was forbidden during the time of mourning. For the Apache, dreaming of a wild animal, or of a destructive fire, or of the return of a dead person indicated that some misfortune was likely to befall the dreamer unless precautions were taken. Apache dream logic sometimes worked in reverse, however. If

Carrying bundles filled with powerful charms, Arikara medicine men return to their village after performing a secret ceremony. Because becoming a shaman required an apprenticeship that could last decades, a man was often well into his middle years before he was deemed a master of the profession.

the action in the dream directly affected the dreamer, the opposite would happen: A person who dreamed he was going to be sick would stay well; a dream about being bitten by a poisonous snake was reassuring, since it meant that the dreamer would never be a victim of snakebite.

Many peoples believed that a part of the human form left the body at night and had experiences in the spirit world; these events were later recalled as dreams. When Jesuit missionaries began living among the Iroquois in the 1600s, they marveled at the Indians' consuming interest in dreams. One missionary wrote: "The Iroquois have, properly speaking, only a single divinity—the dream. To it they render their submission and follow all its orders with the utmost exactness. The Seneca are more attached to this superstition than any others; whatever it be that they think they have done in their dreams, they believe themselves absolutely

Atop a holy promontory overlooking the Grand Canyon, Hopi priests smoke clay pipes and pray for their people. Generally older men, Hopi priests must periodically embark on an arduous journey to survey the boundaries of their nation, stopping at sacred sites to pray and leave offerings.

A PASSION FOR GAMES

Down through the centuries, the rites and celebrations that marked the cycles of life for Native Americans were highlighted by the exuberant playing of sports and games. Few people in history have been more passionately fond of games than the Indians, from rough-and-tumble confrontations on the playing field to forms of darts and dice.

Games themselves began as sacred ceremonies—played to please the gods, to bring the rain down, to honor the dead and comfort the mourners, to encourage fertility, to celebrate success in hunting or war. In

In an 1830s painting by George Catlin, scores of Choctaw women dance in two columns during the ritual always held on the evening before a ball game. At right, tribal elders watch over the piles of blankets and other goods to be wagered on the game by players and spectators.

addition to being spiritually significant, sport fulfilled a practical need for the Indians, teaching by means of athletic endeavor the physical skills that were required of a young warrior and hunter.

Tribes in every corner of the North American continent competed at a number of the same games. The wildest, roughest sport of all was called stickball, which evolved among the Iroquois peoples into what is now known as lacrosse. Versions of stickball were played by tribes everywhere. Widespread, too, was the hoop-and-pole game, as were a great variety of other sports that called for individual skills. All of these activities were played—as many still are—with a zest that mirrored the vitality of Indian life.

In a Catlin portrait, Tullock-chish-ko, the champion Choctaw ballplayer of his time, wears the traditional Indian stickball outfit of breechcloth, beaded belt, long tail of white horsehair, and horsehair collar. He carries the two small, light rackets used in the version of the game played by the Choctaw, Cherokee, and other southern tribes.

Decorated with tassels, the thong-connected balls below and the notched playing stick were made for the Wichita women's game of double ball.

Rackets raised and ready for action, Menominee women charge into the fray during a spirited game of stickball in a painting dating from the middle 1800s. Many tribes barred women from stickball, but several had a tradition of fierce competition between women's squads.

In some tribes, women as well as men battled at stickball, as shown at left, but it was primarily women and children who played two other ball games that were almost as vigorous and rough. One of them, known as shinny, resembled today's field hockey. The object was to knock a ball through the opposing team's goalposts using a special curved stick. Very similar to shinny was double ball, which was played with two balls linked together, the teams hurling these objects forward with sticks. As with stickball, the playing fields could be huge—300 yards long or more—and teams could number as many as 100 on a side.

Five Shoshone women play shinny during the 1990 Treaty Day celebration at Fort Washakie, Wyoming. At right are a shinny stick and baseball-size ball used in the 19th century by Shoshone or Arapaho players. The game may have been the forerunner of ice hockey as well as field hockey.

Poles in hand, Apache players concentrate on a rolling hoop in a rare photograph of the game being played. Below, an 1840s engraving shows Hidatsa men holding a wintertime match of hoop-and-pole while fellow tribesmen look on, bundled in animal hides against the North Dakota cold.

THE RITUAL OF HOOP-AND-POLE

One of the most popular games in North America was the exacting test of throwing skill known simply as hoop-and-pole. A woven hoop—or with some tribes a doughnutlike stone—was rolled across a court that had in most cases been specially smoothed. Charging after it, players hurled poles or darts at the rolling target so that the missiles either hit the hoop or came to rest under it. Often an integral part of religious rituals and credited with power to cure illness, the game was primarily restricted to men; in some tribes, women were forbidden even to watch hoop-and-pole contests.

About five inches across and with a depression in the middle, the round stone below served as the target in the version of hoop-and-pole called chunky, played by southeastern tribes such as the Choctaw.

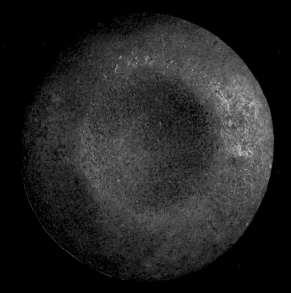

Dating from about 1920, the Cheyenne hoop (above) is made of stiff rawhide strips. A Cheyenne pole (left) of the same era was whittled from a willow sapling. For some tribes, the hoop symbolized the sun's disk; for others, the cycle of day and night.

Hollow deer bones, a length of sinew, and a metal rod make up a ring-and-pin set that was used by the Sioux.

TESTS OF DEXTERITY

Ingenious at making up pastimes, Native Americans created games using bones, sticks, corncobs, and anything else that came to hand. Peoples who resided in cold latitudes took advantage of the snow, inventing a test of skill and strength called snow snake—shown being played by an Iroquois Indian at top—in which contestants hurled polished wooden poles along icy grooves cut into long, molded snowbanks or across a frozen lake. The winner was the player who made the "snake" slide farthest; heaves of more than 300 yards were common.

A similar game involved hurling "bone sliders" along grooves in ice, snow, or even packed earth. The Indians also played dart games using missiles made of corncobs that were thrown at targets laid on the ground. In addition, there was the seemingly simple ring-and-pin game, known from Maine to New Mexico, in which the player tossed a string of connected rings into the air and tried to spear them with a pin as they fell.

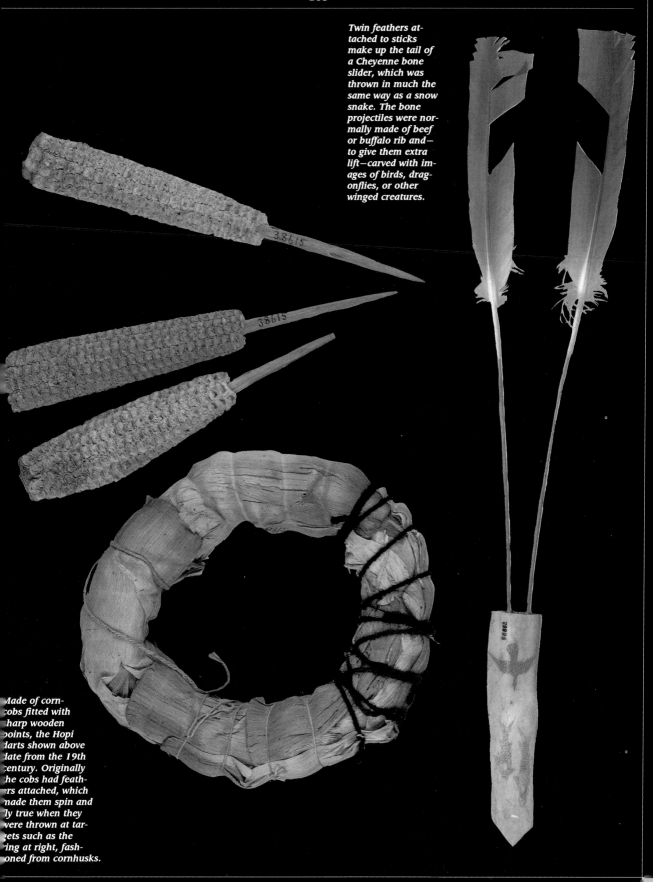

Twin feathers attached to sticks make up the tail of a Cheyenne bone slider, which was thrown in much the same way as a snow snake. The bone projectiles were normally made of beef or buffalo rib and—to give them extra lift—carved with images of birds, dragonflies, or other winged creatures.

Made of corncobs fitted with sharp wooden points, the Hopi darts shown above date from the 19th century. Originally the cobs had feathers attached, which made them spin and fly true when they were thrown at targets such as the ring at right, fashioned from cornhusks.

Playing the moccasin game in Minnesota about 1910, the two Ojibwa men on the right have hidden a ball in one of the moccasins on the blanket; they beat a drum and sing to distract their opponents, who must guess the location of the ball.

Moccasin game equipment used by the Navajo includes a ball, counting sticks for keeping score, and a wand used by players to point at the ball's hiding place.

STROKES OF LUCK

Indians have long played games of chance and skill with the same fervor they devoted to more athletic contests. To many, the outcome of such games did not depend on luck or personal talent but on psychic powers obtained through communion with the gods. Players would perform rituals designed to improve their ability to make a correct guess even when no clues were available. Gambling, popular among most tribes, has usually accompanied such games. But at times they have served a more significant purpose—played in the presence of a sick person, the game was thought to have healing powers.

Dice used by the Sauk and Fox, including two pieces shaped like turtles, rest in a bowl used for tossing them. The best throw of all was to make a turtle land upright.

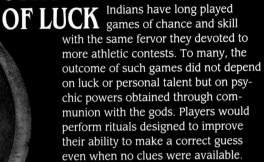

A team of four Shoshone women play the Indian hand game, the one in dark glasses using a blanket for concealment while passing two small bones (like the ones shown at right) between her hands. The opposing team (not shown) had to guess which hand contained an unmarked bone. The spectators wagered on the outcome of the game.

Sitting in a circle, Mohave Indians gamble at cards near an earthen lodge in 1883. On the cards shown below, made of thin rawhide by Apache artisans about 1885, stylized war clubs, cups, coins, and swords replace spades, hearts, and the other European suits; lacking eights through 10s, the deck numbers only 40 cards.

Members of a Sioux high-school basketball team on South Dakota's Rosebud Reservation grasp the school's staff, a symbol of group unity, before a game. The feathers represent the team's victories; the circular ornament, adopted from the Ojibwa, is a dream catcher, an object made to filter out bad dreams and other noxious influences.

ADAPTATIONS FROM WHITES

Native Americans have taken up several games invented by whites, such as playing cards and basketball, illustrated here; they have given each acquisition a special twist, however, to infuse the game with Indian spirituality and symbolism. Consequently, an Indian basketball team might preface its games with a ceremony designed to procure spiritual help in obtaining a victory. As for playing cards, introduced early by the Spaniards to the tribes of the Southwest, the Indians devised their own decks, changing the suits to reflect tribal life and custom.